8-95

D1278922

A Love Affair With The U.P.

A Love Affair With The U.P.

Copyright 1988
by Cully Gage
and
Avery Color Studios
Au Train, Michigan 49806

Written by Cully Gage (Dr. Charles Van Riper)
Cover Photo by Hoyt Avery

Library of Congress Card Number 88-82926
ISBN 0-932212-59-X
First Edition - November 1988
Published by Avery Color Studios
Au Train, Michigan 49806

Table of Contents

FOREWORD

I must immediately warn you that this is not another one of my Northwood Readers. In the five of them that I have written I sought to tell the tales of the fascinating characters I knew as a boy during the early years of this century in Tioga. This one, instead, is about the land, the forest, lakes and streams of the Upper Peninsula of Michigan, and how they shaped one man's life.

Because words alone cannot possibly capture the beauty of that lovely land, I sought the aid of some fine friends to provide the illustrations for my narrative to augment my own, so this is their book as well as mine. I thank them all for their kindness.

Cully Gage
2821 Milham
Portage, MI 49002

Contributions From My Friends
Photocredits
Listed by Page Number

Jean Bogetto: Cover, 12, 54, 59
Andy Amor: 9, 10, 25, 35, 40, 48, 50, 56, 65, 105
Diane Brandstetter: 37, 39, 44, 45, 46, 52, 77, 84
Dennis Visserink: 26, 43, 91, 100, 102
Reino Kangas: 15, 17, 33, 66
Amy Van Ooyen: 69, 92
Cathy Squires: 11, 64, 67, 95
Wayne Premo: 53, 82, 83
Tom Avery: 22
Gregory Winn: 75
Dick Marshall: 98
Richard Waisanen: 106
Ron Avery: 29
Hoyt Avery: 99

My Boyhood In The Forest

One more day! Just one more day and my father would have to return to Tioga and his medical practice. He'd been hunting from Thompson's camp at the Boilers for two weeks, without getting a shot, because the weather had been unusually warm with no snow on the ground to show tracks. In other years there had always been many deer around Wabeek Lake but this time he'd only jumped three and not one had antlers. Disinclined to hunt that same territory again, Dad decided on that last day to go west instead, although that meant he'd have to traverse an immense swamp full of windfalls and thick brush.

After struggling in that swamp for an hour he at last emerged, to find himself on high ground covered with tall hardwoods, mainly sugar maples, yellow birch and hemlocks. In his old age, remembering, Dad said, "It was almost as though I were in a great park. No underbrush. I could see for miles and there were deer signs everywhere."

Discovering a heavily packed deer runway that was heading westward, my father followed it and suddenly found himself on a high bluff overlooking a lake. "I didn't even know that such a lake existed," he said. "That lake was a vision, the loveliest lake I'd ever seen. Below me was a little sandy beach, so I went down to it, sat on a log, and ate my sandwich washed down with lake water that seemed both pure and very cold. What a sight that was! I've never forgotten that moment."

The Lake my Father Found

9

Dad refilled his pipe. "Wanting to see more of the lake, I walked around its south edge on a deer trail under big cedars. Beyond another little sandy beach a point ran out into the water with great boulders emerging from the surface. Beyond that I came to the south bay surrounded by big hardwoods, and then the west bay where I almost stepped into our big spring. I remember filling my collapsible tin cup and drinking its icy water. Across from me on a rocky ledge was a single big white pine so I had to see that too. Yes, Cully, I remember that trip as though it were yesterday. I knew I ought to get started back for camp but had to see what was around the birch point just beyond me, and there I found the outlet creek in a meadow of tall grass surrounded by firs. Because the meadow was full of water too deep for my boots I skirted around its edge hunting for a place to cross. Finally finding a big beaver dam on the creek where I could do so, I spied the shimmer of big water through the trees, climbed a hill to escape the windfalls and came out on another lake. I felt like Balboa discovering the Pacific."

This second lake was long and narrow with high granite cliffs that plunged into deep water on its southern shore, and opposite the bluffs there was a little rock island surrounded by lily pads. Many rings on its surface showed that it held fish. If anything, it was even more beautiful than the first lake he had found.

Pine Point

Dad said the thought came to him that he should try to buy the lakes and build a cabin of his own on them but that he rejected the idea immediately. Why own land up there when the whole forest was free? Why pay taxes on a lake that had no road to it and perhaps no fish in it? He had free use of Thompson's cabin right on a road up which supplies

10

could be hauled in and the deer hauled out by sleigh or lumber wagon. A crazy idea!

It was time to get out of the woods. Not wanting to tackle the big swamp again my father set a course southeast so he could hit the logging road along Wabeek Creek that led to Thompson's cabin. Just before he came to the high hills above the old logging dam he saw a buck coming around a knoll and shot it, an eight pointer, he said. After field dressing the deer, he dragged it down the hills and hid it beside the road for the teamster to pick up the next morning when they broke camp. "The best day of my life," Dad said.

For several years Dad hunted from Thompson's cabin, always roaming the country around the lakes he'd found, always getting his buck. One year, going around the big lake, he crossed a stream coming from the north, and followed it up to its source, another smaller but even more beautiful lake nestled deep in high hills. Again he thought of buying all of them someday. A crazy, absolutely insane idea!

Dad told me this when in his old age (he lived to be 94), I asked him how he came to buy our lakes. "I really had no intention of doing so," he said, "but after the mine closed and Thompson moved away in 1912 his cabin went to hell. People had left the door open and porkies had wrecked it inside. Then a bear tore off many of the roof boards. Absolutely uninhabitable! So Fred Donegal (Old Blueballs) and I bought a tent and hunted from it for five years, pitching it in Bush's Clearing and up on the West Branch of the Tioga River."

The Second Lake

I remember that tent very vividly because Halstead Donegal and I once joined the two men to stay overnight. It was a great adventure for two boys aged ten and twelve, but never have I known such misery.

11

With about four inches of snow on the ground and temperature near zero, the little tin box stove provided too much heat once the fire got going. It was so hot we cooked in our blankets, but the fire never lasted more than half an hour and then we froze. The men told us that it was our job to keep the fire going all night but Halstead, a fat kid, got up only once to help. I was very skinny then and my one blanket didn't help much so I did the firing. Once I woke my father, saying that the hardwood slab under the stove was smoking, which it was, and that I was afraid the tent would burn up. "Get some snow and throw on it," he growled, "and leave me alone." It was a long night.

After four or five years of hunting from a tent my father got fed up with firing all night or perhaps he kept thinking about the lakes he'd discovered. Anyway, he decided he'd have to build a cabin by those lakes. Always a very frugal man, he got some friends of his from Ishpeming to join him in the project. Dubious at first, they were completely convinced one summer when he took them up to the lakes and they saw eleven deer.

One of the men was Captain Keese, head of all of the Oliver Mining Company's properties in the area, who provided two carpenters and a teamster and some men to hack out a wagon road. In just three days the road was cut and the cabin erected. Most of the lumber and the corrugated iron sheets for the roof came from our closed mine but the logs were cut on the site. Dad furnished the cooking and dinner ware from his old hospital and also the bales of straw for the four double bunks, straw that many generations of mice came to appreciate until we finally threw it out and brought in mattresses.

The Old Cabin

The cabin, like most of the hunting and trapping cabins of the time, was built low to the ground to conserve heat but with dimensions of twenty-four by fifteen feet it was much larger than most of them. From the front it really didn't look like much, just logs and a short door, a very short door. Anyone who ever stayed there was sure to thwack his head on the upper door frame sooner or later. Once, after an absence of several months, I returned to find a rueful message scrawled on birchbark above the door: "Bow before entering!" Twice that short door saved the life of wild critters. Once, when the men were eating lunch, one of them spied through the east window a buck coming down the wagon road. Grabbing their guns, three men got stuck in the door and of course the deer got away. The same thing happened again one moonlit night when a Canadian lynx crawled out on a big maple limb that hung over the cabin and let out its unearthly howling. Yes, it was a small door.

I've only heard the sound they heard that night three times in my life and each time it lifted the hairs on my scalp. The first time was when Mullu and I were exploring the Haunted Whorehouse, an account of which I've written in my book *Heads and Tales*. The second time occurred when Jim Johnson, my father and I were sleeping by a night fire at the headwaters of the Tioga River. We had caught a lot of brook trout and the baskets were hanging on a branch above my head, when suddenly the silence was shattered by a series of bloodcurdling howls. It sounded like a woman screaming in mortal agony. To make it worse, Jim howled back with a similar scream from his blanket behind me, and I almost jumped out of my skin. I sure kept the fire burning strongly all the rest of that night.

The third time was even worse. I'd been fishing up on the east branch of Wabeek Creek and was walking back to camp just before darkness set in, when I heard that terrible yowling close behind me. I opened my knife and quickened my pace only to hear it again and again. Well, that lynx followed me all the way to camp and I slammed the door shut in a hurry. I knew that lynx had never been known to attack a man, but remembering that long walk in the darkness I still feel the shiver of terror crawling up my spine. Although I never did see the big cat, I sure heard a lot of him.

I asked my father once why he'd selected the site for the cabin on top of the steep hill rather than down at the edge of the lake. He replied that he wanted to hide it so others wouldn't know it was there, and besides in the morning when he set out to hunt he didn't want to climb that hill. Because there was no well and all our water had to be hauled up in buckets, that didn't make much sense. Besides, people saw the new road immediately and had to see where it went. Just one year after the cabin was built, eleven of them had written their names on the wood fiber plaster that chinked its logs. Nevertheless it was a lovely spot that he'd selected. Huge virgin maples all around it towered into the sky and many large stones covered with moss were everywhere. To enable the teamsters to turn their rigs around, a little clearing was created directly in front of the cabin and from it, if you looked closely, you could see the lake.

In 1917 when the cabin was built, my father did not own any of the land around his lakes. Indeed he didn't know who owned it nor care. Back then the forest belonged to everyone, or so we felt. The whole U.P. was dotted with cabins built by men who didn't possess a square foot of it. There were no "No Hunting" or "No Trespassing" signs. When Cyrus McCormick, the millionaire from Chicago, put up a steel gate across his entrance road someone shot off its hinges, hauled it half a mile and threw it in the river. Hunting cabins were never locked, so that anyone who needed shelter could have it, and always there was coffee and korpua in a mouseproof can to be freely consumed. It's big country up there. One could walk forty miles north and never cross a road until he came to Lake Superior. Lost souls needed food and shelter.

Although many changes have come to the U.P. in the eighty-two years since I was born, the huge wilderness that was ours still remains. From a plane it is still a vast forest of green dotted by innumerable lakes and streams, and the hardy people who live in it still have that wonderful feeling that it is theirs. They can hunt in it, fish in it, or just walk in it without ever having to get permission. No wonder youths born in the U.P. leave it reluctantly when they have to go Down Below to get jobs; no wonder they dream of it and return when they are old.

Now we can drive a car right to the water's edge of our big lake but back then it wasn't so easy. Leaving Tioga, you drove your horse and buckboard west, crossed the Tioga River on a log bridge, then started up The Grade. This was an old railroad bed that had once run northwest all the way to Lake Superior, a speculator's folly that was abandoned almost as soon as it was completed. When I was a boy, the iron rails had been removed but many of the wooden ties had not, so it was a rough, jolting ride, but a beautiful one because the road by the river was lined with huge granite hills. Dad told me that when he first arrived in the U.P. in the late 1890s the whole valley of the Tioga was almost barren of trees because of the forest fires that had followed the logging off of the great white pines in the 1880s but, by the time I was old enough to roam that river, the forest had healed itself. Fortunately the railroad bridges had not burned and we had to cross four of them before turning off on the logging road up Wabeek Creek. Built of heavy pine timbers with iron cables between the uprights, they were still solid enough, but sometimes we'd have to get off the buckboard and lead the horse across the open spaces between the railroad ties. One of the bridges had a heavy rope dangling from one of the cables and was called "Hangman's Bridge". There were tales of a lynching that had occurred there but I never could learn the details.

Just before the fifth old railroad bridge we left The Grade and drove along a good logging road that followed Wabeek Creek, one of the many tributaries of the Tioga. It wasn't really a creek but a small river ranging in width from ten to twenty feet. At spring breakup or after heavy rains it could become a deep torrent of rushing water, and in the old days they had floated pine logs down it, using the lake of water stored in Wabeek Dam three miles upstream. When our cabin was built that logging road was in pretty good shape because it hadn't been many years since the last log drive. Dad told me that when I was seven he and my mother had driven up one afternoon to watch the rivermen break open a large log jam that had formed in the gorge where the present road leaves the plain and winds up into the hills. He said it was really exciting to see the rivermen with pikepole and peavy running out on the floating logs and prying on the key log, then leaping from log to floating log when it finally broke loose. I wish my parents had taken me along with them that afternoon.

Old Railroad Bridge on The Grade

Not far below Wabeek Dam the old logging road crossed the Wabeek at a ford in some rapids. No bridge, just a relatively shallow place, and just beyond that ford our new cabin road turned sharply left, ran along the base of the big hills, climbed a very steep one, and made its way through heavy woods to the cabin. Dad said he could hear Pete Theriault, the teamster, yelling at his big draft horses as they hauled the lumber wagon with camp supplies up that first hill, although it was half a mile away. "Gee, Maude! Sacre Bleu! Get over dar, Margrette! En avant! Whoa! Haw, Maude! Wot a road this, n'est ce pas! A beaver, she could make a better wan!" Over the hills and through the swamps they came, over the rocks and windfalls, but By Gar, they always made it. Oui!

Then, like every good teamster, old Pete would have to get the hay and oats out of the wagon and, cursing, carry up many pails of water from the lake for his team before entering the cabin for his shot of whiskey, tea and sandwiches. And talk! Always shouting, even there in the cabin, Pete was prone to a bit of distortion now and then. Once he told of shooting four deer without even getting out of his wagon. "Taow! Taow! Taow!" he roared. "Four deer!"

Dad interrupted. "But, Pete, you only shot three times. How come four deer?"

"Never you mind, Doc. Four deer!"

Hauling Supplies to Camp

Then came the unloading. Two large blue hampers filled with blankets and clothing, bread, pies and cookies came off the lumber wagon first, then a large wooden box (which we still use as a woodbox), holding the canned goods, meat, two water pails filled with eggs each wrapped in newspaper, two big slabs of bacon and a ham. One year a crate of squawking chickens sat on top of the load.

For over a decade six men lived in that cabin for two hilarious weeks beginning on the first of November, which was when deer season then began. Freed from the cares and responsibilities of jobs and families, they acted like kids just let out of school.

Besides Captain Keese and my father, the other four Regulars (as they called themselves), were Jim Johnson, Tom (Swede) Ackman, Tony Marchetti and Lou Toutloff, an unusual mix of characters. Let me tell you about them.

Old Cabin In Winter (Front View)

Jim Johnson, the caretaker of the mining properties around Tioga, had been a lumberjack, a lumber camp boss, and a sheriff. Though very soft-spoken he was tough and fearless. Once, when an inmate from the state prison at Marquette had escaped and was reported to be armed and dangerous and walking the railroad track by Clowry east of town, Jim, posing as a railroad worker with a shovel over his shoulder, went out to meet him. Jim just nodded casually when they met, whirled around as they passed, clobbered the escapee with his shovel, and dragged him back to town. No big deal!

I liked Jim a lot. He was my father's fishing partner too and occasionally I was permitted to join them on a trout fishing expedition. Only once had I ever seen Jim without his usual calmness. Camping overnight on a bluff above Brown's Dam on the Tioga to get away from the mosquitoes, we'd built a little fire and spread out our blankets. The men, of course, had the best mossy spots near the fire, while I was relegated to a hard place away from it. Fair enough. Boys were low on the pecking order. Suddenly Jim and my father, almost in unison, jumped up yelling, tearing off their clothes and beating themselves. They had bedded down in a large red ants' nest, the terrible little critters the French Canadians called pissants whose bites are like living fire. Lord how those two naked men danced in the moonlight and cussed, as I hid my head under my blanket to stifle my laughter. Yes, I always liked Jim Johnson. He always treated me like a man and told me wondrous tales of the old logging days.

The second of the other regulars, Lou Toutloff, owned a drugstore in Ishpeming, and was a jeweler on the side. A short man with a Russian accent and gold-rimmed glasses, he was the camp cook, a very very good one, Dad said. Rarely doing much hunting, but creating one masterpiece after another on that old wood range, he also had a million jokes that kept the crew laughing.

Tony Marchetti was the third of the Regulars. A short, wiry Italian, he was the strongest man in camp. Dad said that Tony could sling a big buck over his shoulders and carry it for half a mile through rough country before putting it down to rest. Having been a timber cruiser for a big logging company, he was very woods-wise and an excellent shot. Once when I was up there Captain Keese threw a whiskey bottle high in the air and Tony hit it in the air on its way down - with his rifle. You had to be very good to do that. He and my father were the only really serious hunters in camp. They always got their own deer and some for the others who spent most of their time playing poker and drinking.

Finally there was Tom (Swede) Ackman. A very tall man with scattered brown teeth from a lifetime of snuff, he had the biggest beak of a nose I've ever seen on anything but a horse. Tom's role was to cut the firewood and haul the water and to be the butt of the many practical jokes that always characterize a deer hunting camp. Once, when Dad was painting a little knife-cut with mercurochrome, a bright scarlet ointment, Tom said that he had a little cold and asked him if the stuff would be any good for it. "Of course," Dad replied and he painted that huge nose from stem to stern before telling Tom that it was indelible. Dad said Tom didn't need to wear his red jacket out in the woods, that one could see that nose a quarter of a mile away.

In his old age my father liked to tell about the horseplay and the tricks the Regulars played on each other up there in the old days. One of them occurred even before the cabin was built. Captain Keese, who was averse to physical work but not to command, ordered Lou Toutloff to dig the camp cellar. "Four by four and four feet deep," he said. It was to be used to store the potatoes, rutabagas and other stuff so they wouldn't freeze. Now, digging such a hole in the tangled roots and rocks was rough going but Lou made a beginning, then called Captain Keese aside and showed him a little piece of ore in his shovel. "That's gold ore," said Cap. "Don't tell the others about it and give me the shovel." Not until he'd finished digging did Lou tell him that he'd gotten the gold sample from the Ropes Gold Mine near Ishpeming.

Just two other anecdotes among many: Each of the four bunks in the cabin was wide enough for three men, but the lower ones were reserved for Jim Johnson and Tom Ackman because it was their job to keep the fires going all night. Dad and Captain Keese shared the upper bunk by the window, Dad sleeping next to it with his watch, flashlight and glass of water on the sill. Directly below him was where Tom Ackman slept. Rather than having to climb over the huge bulk of Captain Keese when Dad had to take a pee at night, he did it in an empty whiskey bottle. Tom told my father to be careful and not spill, so of course Dad emptied his glass of water so it dripped on the old Swede's face.

Three of The Regulars

An even worse one: One evening after the men had finished a fine meal and were waiting for dessert, Lou told Tom to bring in some more cut wood before he served the raisin pie fresh from the oven. When he was gone, the men watched while Lou carefully inserted a black deer turd into Tom's slice of pie. Oh how the men laughed when Tom smacked his lips and said it was the best raisin pie he'd ever eaten -until Lou told them he'd put one in each of their slices too.

When the Regulars were in camp, my only visits up there came on the weekends when I drove old Billy, our white horse, hitched to the buckboard to bring up mail, any messages phoned to my mother, and a stack of Chicago Tribunes. Occasionally I also brought up fresh milk and a few other supplies. Though the horse was spirited, I could handle the reins well and the trips were a great pleasure to me. Also when I got to the cabin the men treated me as though I were one of them, fed me ham sandwiches so thick I could hardly bite into them, and gave me tea that was so black and strong it had a coppery taste. I never saw my father because he was always out hunting. After a big breakfast Dad would hit the trail with only an apple and a hunk of bologna in his mackinaw and never return to camp until dark unless he'd shot a deer.

One year, skipping school, I got to drive up there in the middle of the week. Lou Toutloff had walked to town to say that they'd gotten two bucks they wanted me to bring back to put in our icehouse, because the weather was turning warmer and they were afraid the deer would spoil. I sure felt proud to have the responsibility and hoped the other kids would be out of school to see me driving that buckboard.

Let me say something about that icehouse. It had originally belonged to the hospital, but every February it was refilled with ice from Lake Tioga. It was fun to watch the men cutting that ice. First they scraped the snow from the surface until they found blue ice, then scored it so it would provide chunks three feet long and a foot wide. Usually by that time the ice was about two feet thick or more. How that ice saw sang in the frosty air as the men pumped it up and down cutting along the lines. Then came the fitting of big tongs to the blocks and skidding them up on the sleigh.

Always the next day I went back to the place, cleaned out the slush ice, and fished for lawyers, a landlocked codfish with a long fin running all along its top and bottom. They were very ugly, easy to catch and fine eating. The fish never fought at all and when I flopped them onto the ice they froze instantly. My mother always hated to cook lawyers because even though they were cleaned and cut up they always jumped around in the frying pan as they thawed.

Before I hitched Billy to the buckboard I checked the icehouse to see if it were cool enough. It was all right. There still were two layers of ice blocks in the sawdust because we'd had a cool summer and the charcoal within the double walls had preserved them. Yes, the deer would keep well in there.

Driving up to camp was a delight. As Billy trotted along The Grade, I felt like a king high on the seat of the buckboard. The Tioga was in flood with curls of white foam over every hidden rock and only patches of snow remained in the woods. It would be a warm day. Crossing the Wabeek at the ford caused no trouble, and we made it up the steep hill without difficulty. I let the horse rest for a moment at its top, then let him walk the rest of the way to the cabin, dodging the many rocks and logs. It was a rough road but we made it. When we got to the little clearing in front of the cabin, I backed the buckboard around expertly so the horse would be facing the swamp road again, whereupon Tom Ackman told me I could sure handle a horse, which pleased me mightily. Taking off Billy's bridle I gave him hay and oats from the back of the buckboard and brought him a pail of water from the lake. Then the men invited me inside and gave me some milk and two big hermit cookies. Again Dad was out hunting, but I left some Tribunes and mail for him and a note saying "Be sure to get Old Napoleon, Dad."

After I put the bridle back on Billy the men began to load the two big bucks into the box of the buckboard. Knowing that there might possibly be some trouble, one of the men held the bridle firmly as I climbed up on the seat and picked up the reins for the trip home.

They got the first buck, a ten-pointer into the buckboard without difficulty, but when the second buck which had been killed early that morning was slung on board, Billy went crazy. The smell of blood! He broke away from the man holding him, reared upward, kicked at the shafts and took off. Fortunately, one of the men jumped aboard, grabbed the reins and yelled at me to hold on. Down the road through the swamp we went careening from one side to the other. Lord, what a ride! Why we didn't break a wheel or why Billy didn't break a leg I do not know. With his ears laid back and his eyes white with terror, he tore over those rocks and logs as though he were insane. Though I clung as hard as I could to the bouncing seat, there were several times when my legs were in the air until the man grabbed me and slammed me back down. Down the steep hill we thundered, almost overturning at its bottom where the road went east, then across the river with a mighty splashing. Horse power! I'd had no idea how strong Billy could be. However, by the time we came to The Grade he was tiring and had stopped snorting. Only then did I see that the man beside me was Tony Marchetti. Reining Billy to a halt, he said, "Damned near sawed his mouth off but he'll be all right now." Handing me the reins, he jumped off, and I sure hated to see him go, but the horse was plumb worn out and I had no trouble with him all the rest of the way home.

That first hunting season Captain Keese got lost three times, so he ordered Jim Johnson to spend the summer building and blazing trails so that wouldn't happen again. One trail ran east to the Ox-Bow on Wabeek Creek near the Boilers, with a branch trail to the old logging dam; The other went west along the hardwood hills, then north to cross the outlet creek and east again to circle the rest of the lake. It too had a branch trail, one that went to Rock Dam on the Tioga.

Jim did a fine job, blazing big trees on both sides so deeply that some of them can still be seen sixty years later, and he cut the paths so they would have the best vistas for hunting. Captain Keese never got lost again, but he complained bitterly that Jim had put the trails over too many hills, especially the first one on the east trail that we called "Out-of-Breath Hill." I remember that hill vividly because I had an experience there that I cannot forget. A heavy deer trail ran along the base of the hill and I was standing there hoping some deer might come along when I heard the wolves.

Back then at the beginning of this century when I was a boy, there were a lot of wolf packs in the Upper Peninsula of Michigan. Often in my back bedroom I would awaken on a winter's night to hear them chasing a deer behind my father's hospital across the street. The wild chorus of their howling always made me shiver though I knew I was safe there under the comforters. In the living room and dining room of my home were two huge wolf skin rugs on the walls, each over six feet long. As children my brother and I would sometimes put our fingers within their monstrous teeth and then run.

Although I was always wandering in the forest, I rarely saw a wolf, but I came across their tracks or kills many times. Often, however, I felt that one was watching me and once I saw one doing it. I'd left my packsack on the sheer cliff overlooking Haysheds Dam and was trying to catch some trout for my supper in the pool below, when suddenly I had that eerie feeling of being watched. Looking up, I saw a magnificent timber wolf right by my packsack. I yelled at it and climbed up the cliff but it was gone. Though my packsack had been overturned, the food had not been touched.

Another time, walking down the railroad track to the Escanaba River I saw a big wolf making its bed at the edge of a swamp. Raising its head, it sniffed for danger in all directions, uttered a long howl, sniffed again, and then curled up in the grass like a dog. Once, when going cross-country to Summit Lake with Arvo Mattila, we suddenly saw a large old wolf lying beside a log not ten feet away. It was dying. Very emaciated and mangy, it managed to totter to its feet, open its mouth in a snarl and growl savagely but we saw in that great mouth only one tooth. I almost had to fight Arvo to keep him from clubbing the poor old critter to death. "Let him die in peace," I said. I still remember the fierce glint in its eyes as it collapsed again beside the log. Those are the only timber wolves I've ever seen in the wilds.

Timber Wolves

As I stood there at the base of Out-of-Breath Hill, the first howls seemed to come from the northwest, about where the stream from our Third Lake enters our big one. There were three of those first howls, each lasting about seven or eight seconds and rising and falling almost an octave. I wish I could find words to describe that howl but I can't. It is wild beyond belief, the essence of the wilderness. No one who has ever heard that series of howls will ever confuse the sound of a wolf with that of a coyote.

Soon after those first howls, another wolf joined in, then another and another as the pack gathered. Then I heard a wild chorus of howls coming from the north edge of our lake, fading a bit as they passed behind the escarpment, then rising in full volume as they came over the pine hill by the sandy beach. Coming directly toward me, they were in full cry with deep howls, high howls, yelping. Standing with my back against a large tree, I had just taken the safety off my rifle when a small doe, fleeing for its life, passed by me not forty feet away. The pandemonium of howling grew louder as the pack came around the base of the hill. Suddenly I heard two sharp barks, then utter silence. I could hear my ears ringing in that silence, nothing else. Tense and alert, I stood there for half an hour but never heard another sound. I suppose the leader of the pack had caught my scent. That was long ago yet I remember it as though it were yesterday. We never hear that wild music now because the wolves are gone. Too bad!

The land around our lakes was first owned by a Thomas Bond and David Gray who purchased it from the government in 1864, paying only $1.25 an acre for the tract. After holding the property for about twenty years they stopped paying taxes and let the land revert to the state after the white pine had been cut, a common practice of that time.

Ours is essentially a climax forest, a hardwood forest, and the pines they cut comprised no solid stand but were scattered among big maples and yellow birch. As a result they were taller and straighter than those of the pine plains. I have measured stumps by our lakes that were over seven feet in diameter, stumps of the prized "cork pines" that could tower almost two hundred feet. In the 1880s most of those in our area had been cut, hauled down to Wabeek Creek, and floated during the spring runoff to Lake Tioga where there was a big sawmill. Just up from the south bay of our big lake are the foundation logs of a lumber camp and horse barns that are now covered with moss and trees and earth. Exploring the site we found bits of old stoves, axe heads, broken saws, peavies and cant hooks - and one half-emptied whiskey bottle. The only pines that were left were those at the edge of the lake, but they cut none of the big hardwoods and for that I have always been grateful.

In 1922, five years after the cabin had been built, my father learned that it had been put up on state-owned land, and moreover that the state was then in the process of selling off a lot of forest property it had acquired through nonpayment of taxes. Foreseeing the possibility that someone might buy the tract and dispossess him, Dad paid off the back taxes and purchased it. He paid more for it than Bond and Gray had but he still got a bargain and finally owned the lakes he'd found so long before.

My father and the other five Regulars hunted from the cabin year after year for almost a decade. Deer season up there was the high point of their lives. The close companionship, the hilarity, the common quest, the freedom from care, all these united them into a brotherhood that only deer hunters can understand.

But, as my beloved Grandpa Gage used to say, "Everything has an end and a woman has two and my uncle Toby could never tell the one from the other." That puzzled me but sadly it is true that all good things must finally end. After almost ten years of joyous annual escape, the era of the Regulars came to a close. Suddenly two of them died in a single year, then two more in the next, leaving only Jim Johnson and my father. When this happened the two survivors stopped hunting from the cabin though they still hunted the land around our lakes. When I asked Dad why, he replied, "Too many ghosts!"

At that particular time I was having a rough time of it in civilization because of a severe stuttering problem. Up there at the cabin I didn't have to talk or suffer the mockery, impatience, laughter and pity that had been my daily fare for years. Strangers had slapped me when I was a small child to break me "of the habit." During my elementary school years I had to fight my way to school and back home because I always slugged any kid who teased me about the way I talked. In high school, recitation was almost impossible and I had none of the boy-girl relationships that characterize adolescence. So I took to the woods.

There in the forest I could talk to the trees and the waves and to the things that went thump in the night. I didn't stutter much to those listeners, only now and then and mildly, if at all. There I found a freedom from anxiety, a pervasive feeling of serenity and great peace as I became a part of the forest, the lakes and the streams. Most of the time I was up there alone. Only occasionally did a few of my friends, Mullu and Fisheye and Tom Hedetniemi, join me, as when I needed their help to build a raft.

During those early years our lakes were full of fish. On a still evening their surfaces were literally covered by rings of rising fish, yet if I wanted some to eat I usually had to hike back to Wabeek Creek to catch a few trout because our lake seemed to contain only chubs, shiners, and other soft fish. These were barely edible though I did cook a few of them when desperate for something besides pork and beans.

During my senior year in High School Dad managed to get two milk cans of fingerling bass from the fish hatchery at Marquette and he, Jim Johnson, and I carried them to the outlet of our second lake. Through tangles of alders and cedars we lugged those heavy cans, one person breaking trail, then taking turns carrying. Only four of the little bass died en route and when we dumped the rest of them in they started feeding immediately.

The Lake

For some years we felt that the planting had failed. Nothing but chubs and shiners got skewered on my hooks. Moreover it was hard fishing for them off the shore because of all the cedars and underbrush, and the raft that Mullu and Fisheye and I had built was almost unmaneuverable when we tried to pole it. Its middle log had never been properly spiked down or tied with baling wire, so I always got a kneeful of water when I stepped on it. Finally the raft disintegrated completely when the ice went out one spring, but by then we had a boat. Captain Keese had it built because he'd shot a deer by the outlet that came from our third lake and it took four men all day to drag it back to the cabin. "Boat?" said Jim Johnson when he first saw it being loaded onto a lumber wagon to take to camp. "That's no boat. That's a bateaux, the kind we used to carry the cook shack down the Fox River in Wisconsin." Nothing more than a long box, built by mining carpenters of heavy planks and tarred at the seams, it must have weighed half a ton.

Nevertheless, it was a boat and though very difficult to row with its fourteen-foot oars, I used it to explore all the shoreline and also as a fishing platform. One dark night, fishing for bullheads that bite better after dark, I built a fire in an old dishpan and put it on the floor of the scow. Though I caught a lot of the fish in the deep hole by the deadhead log, I also burned a hole in the boat which defied patching. Dad gave me hell and I didn't do much lake fishing for some years.

Instead, most of my summers during High School were spent exploring. I hungered to know that wilderness so I might mystically become a part of it, and you can't identify with the unknown.

25

Beginning with the area east and south of the cabin, I roamed the woods, first following the trails Jim had blazed, then just wandering on my own. It was like hearing a symphony for the first time with one surprise unfolding after another. What was over that next hill? What was around that swamp? Where did that little stream run? Gradually I learned the lay of the land and the landmarks that defined it, the big stump in which I sat as in an armchair watching two grouse make love, the bear's den with its last winter's droppings, the hill crowned by huge hemlocks with their branches high above, the pure white vein of quartz on the side of that bald granite hill. I began to name those landmarks. One was *The Old Woman Who Lived in a Shoe*, a huge spruce tree surrounded by fifty little ones. Another was the *Raven Tree* from which I watched a mother raven kick out her last offspring so it would learn to fly. Another was the *Hill of Holes*, a large mass of tumbled boulders with little caves between them full of animal tracks. I learned where the deer trails ran and where they went. In one upland swamp there is still a spot in the tall grass where I came across a spotted little fawn. I found that spot again last summer, fifty years later. Yes, I came to know that part of the forest very well.

Spotted Fawn

In subsequent summers I similarly explored the rest of the land around our lakes, tracing the stream from the beaver dam to its origin in springs that flowed from a hill beyond Porcupine Bluff. I investigated all the hills and swamps between the Tioga River and the Wabeek, always discovering new things. Atop the big granite hill overlooking Rock Dam on the Tioga, I spent hours watching a pileated woodpecker, the cock of the woods, carve a nesting hole in a tall poplar. Lord, its chips were as big as those I could chop with an axe, and I marvelled that the bird didn't bang its brains out. Going around the steep bluffs on the south side of the second lake, I then followed its outlet creek down to the big river, then returning went around its north side to find a huge beaver dam on a tiny creek not more than a foot wide. Near the beaver house was the stump of a white birch tree almost two feet in diameter that the beavers had felled, and the chips from their gnawing were almost as big as those of the pileated woodpecker. Another day found me exploring the creek that came from the Third Lake to enter our big one, discovering that at one place it ran underground, or at least under a canopy of heavy moss from which a mink and two little ones emerged.

Well, that's how those years of my boyhood passed. Day after day I'd set out after breakfast and rarely return until almost sundown. On hot days, and the U.P. always has a few of them, I'd roam the forest clad only in shorts and there were rainy days when I went naked except for shoes, letting the rain pour down on me as it did on the forest floor. Now at the age of 82, there are times when I wish I were that boy again.

Beaver Dam

The Dark Years Of My Youth

The decade after I graduated from High School was the darkest one of my long life and, looking back, I see clearly that the healing power of the forest was what enabled me to survive.

I didn't want to go to college. I wanted to be a bush bum all my life, but my father had other ideas and he won. Feeling that I was stuttering too badly and that I was too immature to go to his alma mater, the University of Michgian, he insisted that the Normal School in Marquette was the place for me.

It wasn't! I've had a lot of tough years but that first one at the Normal was the hardest. I hated every moment of it and my stuttering became much worse, with grotesque head jerks and gasping so severe my listeners thought I was epileptic or insane. Although I avoided speaking as much as possible, there were many times when I could not, and then Dr. Jekyll became Mr. Hyde, with all of the consequent penalties and rejections. At first I'd take the train home each weekend so I could go to the woods to lick the wounds of the week, but soon my father put a stop to that. "You can't run away," he said. "You have to cope." Robert Frost once wrote that "Home is where, if you go there, they have to take you in." When I couldn't go home to my beloved forest and lakes and streams, I became so depressed I'd sit and stare at a bare wall for hours. It was a bad time.

Since the Normal School's purpose was to prepare teachers, I had to enroll in a teaching curriculum. Me a teacher? Lord, I couldn't even ask a waitress for a cup of coffee. Thinking that engineers wouldn't have to talk as much as teachers, I enrolled in a course in Mechanical Drawing. Although I wasn't very good at the drafting table, I did manage to turn in, for the final examination, a credible blueprint of a pump. For that examination we could pick any piece of machinery we wished, prepare our pencilled drawings of it in all perspectives, then make a tracing, and finally a finished blueprint.

The next day the instructor called me into his office with another student, showed us two identical drawings of that pump, and asked us to go to our desk to bring back our original drawings and tracings. When I did so, mine were gone. The other student had his. He'd carefully erased my name from the pencilled drawing and made a new tracing with his name on it. He said he just couldn't understand why there were two identical drawings of that pump. Indeed he sounded so honest and plausible whereas I stammered so badly I couldn't blame the instructor for believing him. The teacher was furious. "It's not just that you did this barefaced cheating," he roared at me, "but that you thought I'd be so stupid I wouldn't discover it." And a lot of other things, one of which was that he'd take immediate steps to expel me.

Stunned and overwhelmed, I was helpless. My father was an honest man, a very honest man. To him any form of cheating was a venal sin. Were I expelled for cheating he would feel disgraced forever. What could I do? Where could I flee?

I fled down to the breakwater in the harbor and jumped off the end of it into Lake Superior. I wanted to die but the shock of that ice water, and instinct, I suppose, made me swim back to the breakwater's huge stones. I sat on them for a long time, weeping. I had even failed at failing.

Breakwater In Marquette Harbor

As it happened I never did get expelled. A classmate who had his desk beside mine testified in my behalf that he had seen me do the drawings and had pointed out an error that appeared on the other student's blueprint. In the end, the instructor felt that there was just enough doubt to jeopardize his case for expulsion. "I'll give you a D in the course," he told me, "but don't you ever try to take another course in my department." Sixty years later, I wish I could thank that student for his despicable deed. I would have made a lousy engineer.

I was profoundly affected by the experience and a few days later, school being out, I was up at the old cabin. But, for the first time, the forest and streams and lakes failed to heal my hurt. Walking the forest trails, I kept reliving the trauma over and over again. Suicidal thoughts kept recurring. How could I ever make a living, stuttering so monstrously? All of the frustrations, rejections and mockery I'd experienced kept revolving through my head. I could not eat or sleep. I was naked in a world full of sharp knives.

Hoping to get some sleep by utterly fatiguing myself, I decided to explore the West Branch of the Tioga to its source. An area that I had never been in, it proved to be rough going, and by the time I came to Rolling Mill Dam I was completely exhausted, so much so that I didn't even eat any of the korpua I had in my pocket, but lay down on a flat ledge above the river.

I don't know how long I slept there, but I awakened to find a starry sky slowly vibrating with the Northern Lights, the aurora borealis. Of course I'd seen them before, as all of us in the U.P. have, but the display that night was spectacular. Great fans of green, yellow and pink light rose from the northern horizon sweeping upwards and shifting from side to side across the sky. As one of them faded, another took its place. I felt as though I were watching some cosmic artist at work using God's paintbrush.

I didn't sleep much the rest of that night, fearing that I might miss something, but in the morning I was rested and at peace. Past hurts had vanished; the anxiety about my future had been erased. Only the present moment had any meaning and I was there by the river in the land I loved. So I followed the stream to a beautiful lake which then had no name, washed my skin and soul in its clear waters, and slept that night on a great mound of brakes (bracken, the short ferns that appear in any spot of the U.P. that gets some sun.) Alas, there were no Northern Lights that night but it didn't matter. I was healed and whole again. I've never really been able to understand why or how this curative process works. All I know is that it has happened to me again and again.

Breakfast

Grandpa Gage taught me a little rhyme that vividly characterizes the decade of my life after I graduated from High School. It went like this:

"It's a helluva life," said the Queen of Spain.
"Three months of pleasure and nine months of pain.
Three months more and I'm at it again.
It's a helluva life," said the Queen of Spain.

Those years are difficult to recall, at least the nine months of them that were spent going to college and teaching. I went to the University of Michigan, got my B.A. degree, taught two years at Saline, returned to get my masters, then taught another year in Tioga. How could I teach, stuttering so severely? I don't know. I worked out ways of silent teaching and made the students do most of the work by doing interesting projects that I had devised. How did I happen to be hired in the first place? It happened because I was still drunk and relatively fluent after a night of drinking the moonshine that John Voelker had brought me to celebrate my winning a poetry prize in a contest judged by Robert Frost. He also brought a roll of toilet paper entitled "POETIC LICENCE." The superintendent who interviewed me was sure surprised that fall when he discovered my impediment but because I taught well, he didn't fire me. I survived, but at the cost of utter misery. Only by dreaming of the forest and lakes and the old cabin was I able to endure. Only by knowing that I could return to them for three months each summer was I able to cope.

I did, however, acquire two good things besides an education: an ancient Model-T Ford named She-bang because of its frequent backfirings, and an equally old canvas-covered wood canoe. Purchasing them in Ann Arbor, I was driving northward when I had the only car accident I've ever had. Following closely behind a bus with a very pretty girl in its back window flirting outrageously with me, the bus made a sharp left turn. I did not. Plowing straight ahead, my car hit a tree and both the canoe and I were flung from it into a freshly plowed field. A farmer who had been plowing that field came over and gave me the devil. "Three people have been killed on that curve," he said. "Are you the fourth?" I said I didn't know and was afraid to find out. But I was just bruised so he called a wrecker and I spent that night, a rainy night, in a chicken coop on the Fairgrounds of Clare, Michigan because I was afraid I didn't have enough money to pay for the repairs, the fee for the ferry, and gas to get home. A lot of chicken lice rode all the way home with me once the car was fixed, but the canoe was all right and so was I.

At first I was unable to find anyone who would help me carry the heavy canoe in to our lakes. It was very heavy with innumerable coats of lead paint on the canvas. I could with difficulty lift it to my shoulders and stagger perhaps a hundred feet before having to put it down, because after the hard winter I was in bad shape physically as well as emotionally. Almost six feet tall, I weighed only 120 pounds of bone and skin. But I used that canoe to explore all the bends of the Tioga and its tributaries.

Once, for three days, I paddled, poled, and carried that canoe up Baraga Creek to the lower Baraga Lake on the McCormick property, catching a lot of the big pike that then were so plentiful. Dad said that the pike probably got up there by going up the Tioga River from Lake Tioga, adding that when he first came to Tioga in 1900 the big lake was full of great northern pike which had originally been brought up there in the tender of a locomotive from Wisconsin. He also claimed that they were not a true northern pike but a cross between it and a muskellonge. As a small boy I watched as my father and Grandpa Gage laid out two of them in our big bathtub that were so long they had to curl at both ends to fit in it. Dad said they weighed way over thirty pounds each.

Twice, when I was a boy, my father let me go with him as he trolled for pike in Lake Tioga. Rowing along the edge of the hardwoods along the north shore of the lake, we trolled a large bucktail spinner on the end of a green braided line that must have been a quarter of an inch in diameter. When a pike hit the lure you had to haul it in, hand over hand, coiling the line neatly in a pile on the bottom of the boat. I remember catching a big one and having the fish thrash around furiously, wrecking my pile of coiled line until Dad hit it over the head with an oar. Catching those pike in Baraga Lake from a canoe was fun.

One morning in late June, after it had rained for many days, I took the canoe up above Rock Dam. The dam at that time was almost intact and the pond above it was almost a lake. Planning a trip downriver in that flood, I examined the old dam carefully to see if I dared shoot through it. It didn't look good. A torrent of black water was rushing through the sluice gate and there was a drop of five feet where it roared off the plank apron. It scared me silly but, after putting a large rock in the front end of the canoe for ballast, I carried the canoe to the pond above the dam, grabbed a paddle and set sail. Down through the dam I went like a bat out of hell! Wahoo! Somehow I didn't capsize, though the canoe whirled around several times before I could bring it under control. Then down that very rocky river I plummeted, paddling desperately to avoid the bigger rocks that rushed toward me one after another. I hit a lot of them and was completely exhausted when I finally came to the taking-out place where the West Branch joins the main river. Folly! Complete folly, but I did it and felt proud that I'd done it. No, I never told my father or anyone what I had done.

After patching its wounds and repainting the canoe, I finally got some friends to help me lug it to the old cabin and the little sandy beach. Compared to the raft and the scow, it was heavenly. To be able to glide across the surface of the lake quietly and with little effort was to open a new dimension of pleasure. No day was complete without a final trip around the lake listening to the night sounds.

People have asked me if I didn't get lonely living up there in the forest so many months each summer. Didn't I miss being with other people? Didn't I ever get bored? The answer was no to all these questions as an account of how I spent my days may explain.

Rock Dam (Low Water)

Living Alone In The Forest

When the sunshine flooded through the east window of the old cabin, I would immediately run down the hill trail to the lake, fling myself into the water, and swim out to the deadhead then back to the sandy beach. If the water was warm enough, I'd just float with the morning sun on my face suffused with the feeling of well being. But it wasn't just a swim; it was a sort of baptism. In that cool clean water I shed all the bad memories of the year before, memories that prowled my mind at night in the form of dreams. For the moment, at least, I was cleansed of all evil. Morning after morning my sin of being a stutterer was washed away.

Then I'd make my breakfast down by the lake where I'd built a little fireplace. Leisurely I'd boil some coffee in a blackened pail, then eat some korpua and a cupful of wild strawberries, raspberries or blueberries according to their season. Oh that wonderful freshness of a U.P. morning! There were times when I wouldn't light my pipe lest I spoil it.

Next I'd take the brown jug I'd found at the site of an old logging camp and paddle over to the big spring in the west bay to get the day's drinking water. Not that our lake water wasn't pure for often I'd use it, but that from the spring was always ice cold and would stay that way in the jug all day. If it hadn't been too long since I'd been in town, I might find there some butter or a mason jar of milk in the cold water. Refrigeration was a problem because occasionally we had some very hot days in the U.P. Not daring to keep fresh meat in the spring because of the animals, I'd usually keep it from spoiling by putting it in a watertight pail which I sank to the bottom of our lake suspended by a rope attached to a float. That worked fine because the bottom lake water was always cold. Even when swimming, if you let your legs down, you could feel the difference.

After I'd filled the brown jug, I always paddled around the lake to see what I could see. Always there were the two loons, sometimes with fluffy little babies trailing behind them. Ravens soared overhead, croaking and occasionally uttering that bell-like gong sound of theirs. A kingfisher plunged from its tree to spear a fish; a great blue heron rose from the outlet marsh flopping its heavy wings; an osprey or eagle circled high above.

Peering over the side of the canoe as I silently glided along, I could see the crooked trails of the clams that lay there on the sandy lake floor with their valves open and undulating slightly, the traceries of crayfish, and the darting shadow of a large chub or perch. On the surface, waterbugs skated erratically. Dragonflies of many irridescent colors dipped into the water, then dried themselves on the prow of the canoe or even on my paddle. Swallows swooped around me catching insects. Every morning I saw something new.

Big Spring

Near the place where the creek from our Third Lake enters our big one I usually saw a deer or two. Because they do not have keen eyesight and seem unaware of danger coming from the water, I was often able to paddle imperceptibly very near them, if the wind were from the right direction. Once I watched a young buck with its antlers still in the velvet spend twenty minutes trying to scrape his horns by rubbing them up and down along a sapling. Before he was done the tree was red with blood. Once I saw a doe teaching her dappled fawn to rid itself of flies by rolling in the mud, then splashing in the lake. Another time, two young bucks pranced about the shoreline, butting heads, danced in the water, then returned to butt heads again. A big buck pawed a bed in the shore moss before lying down to sleep in a patch of weeds, occasionally awakening to stretch its head and sniff before going back to sleep again. I paddled within ten feet of him and he never knew I was there.

We've always had otters on our lakes. Usually they visited me for only a day or two before traveling to other lakes and streams in search of other fish and clams. One morning I observed a whole family of otters sliding down the smooth rocks of Hedet Point having a high old time. They'd climb up to the top of the bluff, then launch themselves downward on their bellies entering the water without a splash, then surface grinning and whistling at each other, then do it again and again. Once two of the younger otters slid down the rock at the same time and when they reappeared they actually hugged each other. I'm sure they knew I was there in the canoe but they were just having fun. At other times I had them swim around my canoe, scrutinizing me with bright curious eyes and an almost human smile behind their whiskers. If I were to be born again I'd like to come back as an otter.

Otters In The Snow

Whenever I came back from my morning canoeing I felt a great peace, the peace that passeth understanding. All my dark thoughts had vanished. Why? I don't know. I just knew that everything was all right. Perhaps it was that with all my senses keenly alert, the concentration of my attention had left no room for anything but the present moment. Up there on the lake there was no past nor future. Time had stopped. I could almost hear my Grandpa Gage yelling, "Enjoy! Enjoy!" in mid air when he fell off the bridge into the pool below.

Deer In Velvet

Grandpa Gage was a great one for projects too. Every morning when he'd shave himself with his straight-edged razor and then my lathered face with the back of it, he would always say, "Now, Mister Muldoon, what, sir, is the pro-ject for the day?" Up there at the cabin I always had a new project that took the rest of my mornings. Perhaps I had to cut dry maple poles for firewood or make a hiding place in a hollow log for my paddles. I recall creating a pearl farm which took several mornings. One day I'd collected a lot of fresh water clams thinking to make a stew of them, and while cleaning their insides I found a little pink pearl. The stew was so terrible I couldn't even eat the potatoes that had been cooked in it, but the pearl gave me an idea. I'd create a pearl farm, make a million dollars and never have to go back to civilization again. Catching the clams was easy. I just had to poke a long stick between the open shells and the clam would grab it tightly. Then I'd pull it out of the water, pry open the valves, put in a grain of sand, and return it. Before I was finished with the project I had four rows of them on the lake bottom with about six clams in a row. Very neat! All of them were still there the following morning, but within a week all had disappeared, leaving only their trails behind them.

Near the clam farm at the edge of the beach was a very tall and hollow pine stub bleached gray by wind and rain and age. Often I'd admired the ospreys and eagles who made their nests in such stubs, so I decided to make one of my own. I spent several mornings nailing rungs inside the hollow trunk, so I could climb up to a little platform on top thirty feet from the ground and be monarch of all I surveyed. One afternoon I was up in my aerie when my brother Joe appeared. "Cully, you have to come to town to vote, Dad says. Have to save the county from the Catholics." I almost fell off my platform laughing at the absurdity of it all. No, I didn't go to town.

For another morning's project, a bit more sensible, I built The Perfect Mousetrap though I certainly didn't wish the world to beat a path to my door. That year, the Year of the Mouse all through the U.P., hordes of the little varmints were everywhere. The old cabin was full of the little buggers both day and night. I set and reset six mousetraps several times each day. The mice would crawl across my face at night; they made nests of shredded paper in my boots; once I found one in the pocket of my pants. I swear that somewhere in the forest they had a mouse factory with an assembly line. Altogether that summer I caught 136 of them.

Tiring of always having to set and reset those traps, I found an old water pail, filled it a third with water, bored holes in the top and bottom of an empty condensed milk can after stripping it of its label, and threaded it on a length of heavy wire so the can would revolve easily. Then I put the contraption across the rim of the pail and rested a stick ladder so the mice could climb up to it. For bait I wound a strip of bacon around the can and smeared it with peanut butter. My reasoning was that the mice would climb the ladder, jump onto the can which would then revolve, dumping the mouse into the water where it would drown. No more setting or emptying traps. All I had to do was to empty the bucket when it got full. Incredibly, the damned thing worked. I enjoyed lying there in the bunk hearing one plop after another. Even Mabel, Pete Half Shoes' pet skunk, couldn't have done a better job.

For another project I made a porcupine graveyard. Back then our woods were infested by them, though now we see very few. Although they were a major nuisance, you weren't supposed to kill porcupines on the theory that a lost and starving man could always club one for food. That theory was in error. A porky can run like hell if it wants to and be clicking its teeth in the top of a tree before you can whistle. They're hard to kill too. You can whop them across the back with a heavy club and they'll only grunt; you have to hit them on the nose, preferably with an axe or shovel, and that's difficult to do when you're barefoot at night and trying to get the bugger that had been raising holy hell on the tin roof. You'd swear it was a bear, such a racket it made. They didn't scare easily. I could yell at them when they were up on the roof and they never blinked an eye. Only by sweeping them off with a long pole could I get them off it, and then before I could grab my axe they were gone up the nearest tree.

One of them almost got me. Returning from fishing one afternoon I found a big porkie chewing on the closed cabin door. While I hunted for a club (the axe was inside) it ran over to a five inch sapling, climbed to the top and sat there grinning. Foolishly I went up that tree to try to shake it off the limb on which it was sitting, but when I was about fifteen feet up the trunk the porky started down, flailing that big tail with its hundreds of barbs from right to left. Letting go, I dropped hard to the ground and cussed as it resumed its perch and grin.

Hungry for salt as that in human sweat, porcupines chewed the handles of my paddles. Once they utterly destroyed a moccasin I'd left on shore as I waded around the east end of our lake. On an overnight expedition, when I awakened in the morning, I found my little aluminum frying pan not only scoured clean but its edges scalloped by their teeth. They love grease of any kind.

The Only Good Porkie Is A Stuffed Porkie

Returning to the cabin after a winter's absence, I found the old cabin a shambles because some visiting hunter had left the door ajar. The porkies had had a ball! Pots and pans had been pulled off the walls and chewed; the chairs were riddled; the table had been gnawed and one of its legs amputated; the bedding in the bunks was foul with their droppings. No, the porcupine is not a very nice animal, even when it's in love. I watched two of them mating, very carefully. First the male urinated all over the female, probably to establish his territory. Then he rose to his haunches as the female, with her tail curled over her head, backed into him and it was all over in a moment of quilled fury. He urinated on her again and slowly ambled away.

As for letting a porky alone so that a starving man could eat it, all I can say is that he'd better have very sharp teeth and be very hungry. I tried to eat the hind quarter of a porcupine once. I parboiled it and fried it and couldn't put a fork into it. Then I boiled it again, roasted and baked it to no avail. When I finally was able to whittle a slice off that hind leg I couldn't chew it. Indeed I couldn't even taste it. So, if you're lost in the woods, suck your thumb rather than try to eat a porky. No, I never liked those critters. Perhaps it takes a porcupine to love a porcupine. So that is why I dug trenches to provide a porky graveyard with a headstone above each. I think I finally had thirteen of the markers as well as a big Indian slate that said "Requiescat in pace." It was a good morning's project.

No, I was never bored up there by the cabin by myself. I built a rock dock so I could get in the canoe more easily; I cleaned out the spring; I blazed a new trail. One morning I clubbed a fool hen (spruce hen) off a limb and baked it in clay over the coals. Those spruce hens are a silly bird. They feel completely safe as long as they are off the ground and you can walk right up to them. I skinned it and salted it and it was good eating, though not as good as a partridge.

Indian Slate

On one rainy day I spent the whole morning trying to blow a series of smoke rings, one through each other, using the black corncob pipe The Regulars had left behind them. (That old pipe still sits in the old cabin and every visitor is obligated to take at least one puff from it.) Anyway,

I once did manage to blow four smoke rings, perfect ones, through each other and, as a consequence, was dizzy for two hours.

Very rarely I did some reading, usually on a rainy day. I'd brought up three books in my packsack: Bartlett's Quotations, Shakespeare's Plays and the Bible. I'd dip into these and then think about what I had read while I made a big birch bark waste basket or something. The forest was far more interesting than any book.

How did I spend my afternoons? They were reserved for roaming. I covered almost every square foot of the land around our lakes and made many crude maps showing the characteristics of the land. Recently I found just one of them, the one that showed The Escarpment northeast of our big lake where a high plateau dips precipitously into a long swamp. The map shows the only two deer trails that descended, and I recall that I never saw a deer track ascending either of them. All of the hoofprints were pointed downward. Just too steep to climb even for a deer but I climbed them just to see if I could.

Eventually, however, I became so familiar with that part of the forest that it lost some of its attraction. I'd been there before. I knew where that little stream went; I knew what was over the next hill. But what was the vast wilderness like north of our lakes all the way to Lake Superior? That I did not know.

Exploring The Wilderness

So the bear went over the mountain to see what he could see. Sometimes these trips of exploratioin would take several days such as the one when I hiked east to Wabeek Lake then north through Hell's Canyon, past the Yellow Dog River, and up into the Huron Mountain Club property. This is a large tract along Lake Superior that has been owned by rich people from Chicago for many years. Including almost all of the Huron Mountains, it was heavily patrolled by guards who were kept busy replacing the "No Trespassing" signs regularly torn off by men from Big Bay. There's something about such a sign that riles the gizzards of the independent people of the U.P. Well, I explored the Huron Mountains and their lovely lakes and caught some trout in their Salmon Trout River. Not that I especially wanted them, but, as Laf Bodine, the best poacher in Tioga, used to say, "It was the principle of the thing."

On another of my solo excursions I spent three days in what is now known as the McCormick Wilderness Tract. Consisting of about five thousand acres, it still contains some of the great virgin white pines because it has never been logged. To walk for days in that virgin forest was to know the U.P. as it used to be. Moreover, it was delightful walking, thanks to the fine trails that McCormick's men had cut and maintained. I met one of his workers on a sunny cool afternoon without a cloud in sight coming down the trail holding above his head an open umbrella of all things. When I asked him why the umbrella, he replied, "What the boss wants, the boss gets," explaining that the multi-millionaire's guests often liked to walk the trails even in the rain and it was his job to make sure that no twig or branch would touch their umbrellas. He said he felt damned silly doing it.

Although I roamed the country on those well-groomed trails from the Baraga Lakes, around White Deer Lake where the McCormicks had their luxurious cabins on an island, then north to the Yellow Dog Falls and Bulldog Lake, I never met another soul. I camped out on Lake Margaret and Summit Lake, catching some big brook trout in each of them, and at the falls where I made the Perfect Balsam bed.

Perhaps you don't know how to make a balsam bed so I'll tell you. First, you cut many armfuls of balsam branches, then cut off the ends of these so each is no more than eight or ten inches long. Then, after laying a log for a pillow, you take each balsam frond and stick it into the ground so it curls over the log. Then you take other fronds and place them so that each one overlaps the one above it. It may take you three hours but will be worth all the effort. Never will you have known such a

42

soft springy mattress from which every movement releases that wonderful fresh fragrance of the deep woods. Just make sure you don't cut your branches too long. I made a balsam bed once for my father and Jim Johnson, and they claimed I'd left "too many bones in the feathers."

The Wilderness

Another time I spent five days going straight north from our lakes to Lake Superior and back, a distance of about thirty miles as the crow flies, though crows don't fly straight and neither did I. You just can't in that big country. I threaded my way over the hills and around the swamps, following a deer trail if I could or just going cross-country if I couldn't. The vastness of that wilderness (about 1800 square miles) impressed me. Often I had the feeling that I was the first human being to have been in that particular place. Certainly I never saw any evidence that anyone had been there before me. Climbing a tall hill, I felt as Father Marquette or Joliet must have felt three hundred years before me, as they saw the green forest stretching to the horizon in all directions.

About dusk I came upon a small lake (Cliff Lake) high in the hills, and made my night camp beside a small rocky stream in a cluster of big white pines and hemlocks. The ground there was almost a foot thick with their needles, so when it began to rain I built a lean-to, covered it with a heavy blanket of the needles, and made a little fireplace in front of it out of flat stones. Completely dry and comfortable in my brown cocoon, I slept so well I hated to leave the next morning.

Shortly after dawn, knowing that I tended to veer to the right, I took a compass course northwest, discovering a good-sized stream, the Little Huron River, and followed along it until I came out on Lake Superior. Oh, the immensity of it, and the intensity too, because on that day great waves coming all the way from Canada were crashing against the shore.

Leaving my packsack near the outlet of the river I spent the day walking eastward along the shore and coming back. At times I had to leave the beach and walk along the highlands because there was no beach, but just a tall outcropping of sandstone against which the waves flung themselves. In other places I could amble easily on wide brown sand feeling the spray on my face. On the lee side of a promontory I found a little cove with a pebbled beach full of stones of various colors. I still have a few of them that I fondle when troubles beset me so that I can know again the peace I felt there.

Pine Tree by Lake Superior

The shore was very clean. Not a can or bottle nested in the sand, and the only human sign I found was a whitened plank among some ancient gray driftwood. Sitting on one of the big boulders I felt that I too had been washed up there on the shore of infinity.

As evening approached, the wind died and the great lake became calm. The huge waves that had charged the shore were gone. Instead, little ripples washed and curled around my bare feet, then retreated,

44

leaving chains of tiny bubbles to show how far they had come. Then dusk came and with it the most spectacular sunset I've ever seen.

I did not build a fire that night; it would have been a desecration. Instead I laid my blanket on the sand. That was a mistake. The soft sand into which I had thrust my toes so many times turned into concrete after I'd lain there awhile. So I moved up to a highland and slept under a single tall pine tree with the moon and stars on my face, to the soft lapping of the little waves below me.

I've since tried to analyze why that great lake had such an impact upon me. I've traveled a bit, walking ocean beaches in Australia, along the lagoons of the Fiji Islands, the rocky shores of the Maine and New Brunswick coast, and along the fjords of Norway and Alaska. I loved all of them but none of them compared with those isolated shores of Lake Superior. Why? Perhaps it is because ocean water is a primordial soup, full of life and the detritus of living things, whereas Gitchee Gummee is (or was) pure. Purity, that was what I felt, pristine purity. It cleanses those who walk along its shores. If you walk or swim in the ocean, you get covered with salt and slime and must wash yourself. If you do so in Lake Superior you come out cold, cold, but clean, clean. Perhaps that is what impressed me so deeply.

Shore of Lake Superior

45

The next morning I dawdled at my little coffee fire reluctant to leave, although my chunk of bologna was half gone and there were only four hunks of korpua left. Still hypnotized by the immense lake, I couldn't bear to leave until I'd seen even more of it. So I walked about a mile or two westward, savoring every step, until I came to a larger river, the Big Huron, where many seagulls met me with shrill and raucous cries. Too deep to wade it without removing my clothes, I finally decided to start home. I had no map. There would have been nothing useful on it anyway, so I just headed south along the Big Huron until it turned west. Over the hills and far away! Let's go home.

The trip back was uneventful except for one scene which has been cemented deeply in my memory. I'd been hiking down a valley full of silvery poplars flirting with me by showing their underskirts in the wind, when I spied a group of deer sleeping in the tall grass of an old beaver meadow. They were all facing away from me and with the wind from the south they never knew I was there. After watching them for a long time, I almost tiptoed my way detouring around them. Peace in the valley!

Deer In Meadow

Again because I'd been veering too far to the right despite my best efforts, I came out of the woods not at our lakes but two miles north on the Tioga River. Close enough! The old cabin put its log arms around me, I was full of fatigue, peace and a bit of triumph. It was good to be home.

One afternoon I decided it was time to really know whether or not our planting of bass in the second lake had been successful, so I took the canoe to the outlet and tried to pole it down the little creek that connects the two lakes. When I found I just couldn't do it because there was not enough water and too many bushes, I tried carrying it on my shoulders but the prow kept hitting branches. Exhausted, I said to hell with it and walked the rest of the way to where a big rock dropped sharply into the lake. Cutting a "government pole" (a long alder branch) I tied on the line and hook I had in my pocket, found one of the four night crawlers that were also in that pocket, put on a bobber, and started fishing.

May I interrupt my tale to say something about catching nightcrawlers for bait? You go out on a dark night, preferably after a rain has soaked the lawn, using a light to spot the little buggers as they lie, stretched out, in the grass. You must walk very slowly, straining your eyes to see the glint reflected by the bodies of those worms, then pounce. Half of the time you miss because they're quick to dive back into their holes and when you do manage to grab one you must pull it out slowly or it will break off. You never jerk; you just tease them out. Occasionally you may get two lovers lying passionately side by side.

All I caught at first in the second lake were two yellow pumpkinseeds and then a four-inch perch. About to give up, I let the perch swim around a bit before leaving, and suddenly a big fish swam up and grabbed it. A bass! A bass! A two-pound bass! I threaded my last nightcrawler on the hook and caught a bigger one. Whoops!

It took three more years before the bass found their way up the outlet creek to flourish in our big lake. Meanwhile, I fished the second lake a lot but it was hard to fish from shore except off the big rocks, so one summer I spent three weeks digging a canal of sorts following the stream between the two lakes. Digging out those Labrador Tea bushes with a pickaxe was hard work and a lot of muck kept seeping back into my ditch, but finally I had it done well enough to be able to take the canoe to the second lake. It was like skiing. I had to stand up in the middle of the canoe and pole it forward with a paddle in each hand when going around the curves.

For about ten years we caught a lot of very big bass as they consumed the myriads of chubs and shiners that had been so prevalent. My biggest one, a seven pounder, I caught on a homemade fly off the steep cliff on the south side of the second lake. I was in the canoe and as I tried to bring in the bass the canoe went to the fish rather than vice versa. I ate on that fish for three days and smoked its great head so I could have some proof of the monster.

Dad never liked fishing from a canoe so he bought a heavy plywood rowboat from Sears and, after my brother and some friends hauled it in to our lakes, he and Jim Johnson often came up with their casting rods and artificial minnows. Those big bass would hit anything thrown at them, but Dad mainly used a Crazy Crawler or a scarred old pikie minnow. I rowed the boat for them and it was fun to watch Dad rearing back and reeling as fast as he could when he had a strike. He never played the fish; just horsed it in.

47

Outlet Meadow - Where I Dug The Canal

After about ten years of that wonderful bass fishing, the bass became smaller and then stunted. There were just too many of them in the lakes. The chubs and shiners had disappeared. I lost interest; the fishing was too easy and the bass were too small. Then suddenly, or within two or three years, we began to catch bigger bass again and also some northern pike. No one had planted these; they must have come up the river from Lake Tioga, then up the stream that flows out of our second lake. Along with the pike came an explosion of the perch population, why I don't know, but they were everywhere. The result was that for over thirty years we had some of the best bass and pike fishing in the Upper Peninsula. The beavers helped too by building big dams across the outlets of both lakes, cutting down many birch trees which fell into the lakes to provide excellent cover, and flooding the marshes for the spawning. In the west bay they had a house that rose six feet above the water, so we saw them often.

The pike became very large from feeding on the small bass and the multitudes of perch. Often they broke our lines. One of them, Moby Dick, became a legend of our lakes. Dad was the first to hook and lose him. I wasn't there at the time but as he told the story, he, my brother Joe and Joe's son, were casting from the aluminum pram by the rocks where our big cabin now stands. (I've forgotten to tell about that damned pram. Only eight feet long and very unstable, Dad had purchased it because the rowboat was always leaking.) Anyway, suddenly Dad had this huge pike on, and after a noble battle brought it alongside the pram and tried to bring it over the edge of the boat. But the pike was so big he couldn't get it over the side, so Dad stood up, lifting his pole high, and over they went into the lake. In his eighties at the time, Dad swam for shore still holding his rod with one hand up in

48

the air but Moby Dick was gone. My father mourned that fish all the rest of his days.

Several of us have had Moby Dick on our lines in the years that followed, but always Moby Dick got away. I still have a big hook that he bent out of shape when he escaped just as I was about to bring him into my canoe. Another time I had him right beside the canoe when suddenly he tore under it, dumping me in the lake too. Once I saw him chasing a two-pound bass that was leaping frantically on the surface trying to get away. It looked like an alligator in pursuit. Must have been forty pounds or more!

That was when I began to fish with a big minnow suspended from a large bobber, a practice I had previously despised. Big pike preferred big chubs over perch or artificial lures, so for years I lugged minnow pails with ten-inch chubs from the Third Lake to fish for Moby every morning and evening. It got so I stopped fishing for bass entirely except when very hungry. Instead I'd paddle over to Moby's haunts off Birch Point or Pine Point and, almost hypnotized, sit there watching the big bobber until the sun came up or went down and I caught a lot of big pike that way. When the bobber would begin to move furiously, I knew there was a big fish underneath it. When that bobber disappeared, I put the reel on free spool because you have to wait and wait. Pike seize the minnow sideways and swim fast far into the lake before turning to swallow it. As the line is being stripped from the reel, you have to tend it so there will be no slack in the line, yet make sure the fish feels no pressure or it will drop the minnow. And then you strike very hard because pike have very bony mouths. It's a tricky business. The alertness and anticipation can be exquisite so I came to enjoy minnow fishing after all. And still do!

I wish I could report that I finally caught Moby Dick but I didn't. For all I know he's still swimming in the deep water beyond Herman's Rock or has died of old age as I will, hopefully not before I finish this account. I know how Captain Ahab felt as he pursued the great white whale. Trying to catch Moby Dick almost became a compulsion. To my shame, I once told my grandson, Jonathan, that Moby Dick was mine. Mine! That if by chance he had him on his line I'd grab the rod away from him. But I failed, as I failed in my other quest - to grow The Perfect Potato. No matter! I had the fun of it. When my father was ninety-four years old, I asked him how he had managed to live so long. He grinned and replied that the days he'd fished and hunted didn't count. If so, I still have a few more years coming to me and, besides, last summer another big fish broke off my line.

Later in that decade I made several other trips across country to Lake Superior, usually with a companion or two because I'd had an experience that taught me a lesson. Hungering to know the country east and south of our lakes, I had made my way up the east branch of Wabeek Creek then across to Log Lake with its little granite islands covered with pines. I had in mind to try to find Old Man Coon's gold mine and perhaps the three heavy jugs I'd seen in his covered spring, as described in my tale Omnium Aureum at the end of my first Northwoods Reader. I didn't find them. I did come across a beautiful little clearing covered with wildflowers backed by the dark green of firs, but no signs of his cabin were in it. Following Klipple Creek northward I found Wolf Lake and then headed back over rough country west to the Wabeek. Hoping to get to the cabin by dark I was hurrying, (a damned fool thing to do in the big woods), when I took a bad fall on some rocks, hurting my knee so badly I could not move my right leg at all. No one knew where I was. The leg seemed completely paralyzed. Trying to crawl, I only made twenty feet before having to quit. As I lay there helplessly, I thought that my suicidal impulses had finally found reality. Well, if I had to die there at the edge of that swamp, at least I would die in the land I loved. Fortunately, after about an hour, I was able to feel my leg again and to move it, so limping painfully I made my way back to the cabin. Until then I'd never had any fear of being alone in the forest. I'd often taken foolish chances, leaping from rock to rock or exuberantly running pell-mell down the steep slope of a granite hill, but after that experience I usually took a companion with me when I made a long trip. I've always hated trying to be wise; I've always liked risks, but I've learned from my many follies.

Log Lake

Let me tell of two more of the trips I made exploring the forest north and west of our lakes. With Iggy Waisanen and George Egland, I first hiked to Summit Lake, then cut northeast to find the headwaters of the Big Huron River. It began to rain terribly hard by afternoon and poured all night and the next morning, as we followed that rocky stream. Finally through the mist we saw a large range of hills running northward, and being pretty sure the river would too, we cut diagonally to intercept it. Suddenly we came onto a large clearing, perhaps forty acres or more, covered with tall grass and in the middle of it we found a big cabin and some fallen-down barns. Evidently someone had tried to homestead there long before. The two-story cabin had been wrecked by porcupines and age, but it had a long box stove and mouse-chewed mattresses upstairs, so we three wet and bedraggled souls felt we'd hit heaven itself. Building a big fire in the stove, we spent that night and all the next day there until the rain quit. I've never been able to find out who owned that cabin so deep in the wilderness, but he must have been a kindred soul, and I thank him for the hospitality.

The next morning after a fine sleep we went our way, discovering a series of waterfalls pouring down a cut in the hills, which made me wish for a camera as all waterfalls always do. We were intrigued to find that all the trout above those falls were brook trout and all those below it were rainbows. At last we came to the big lake, camped there overnight, and then followed the shore to Skanee and the end of Huron Bay. Again I felt the immensity and purity of that great expanse of pure water, but I found myself wishing that I had been alone. My companions talked too much.

On still another expedition Iggy and I followed The Grade to its terminus on Lake Superior. Over and over again we marvelled at the incredible difficulty those early railroad workers had encountered and surmounted. They had erected log trestles half a mile long across huge swamps, built innumerable bridges, and carved out cuts through solid granite. The biggest of those cuts was a seven-mile stretch at the Divide of Land about eight miles from the lake. With only oxen and hand drilling, they had opened a right of way through the granite that was sixty feet deep in places. How they could have hoped that when the snows came a locomotive could have gone through that gorge, was a mystery. Just beyond that deep cut, the land sloped swiftly to the lake, and there the workers had to construct a tall long embankment of rock and fill dirt to elevate the track. Walking along that stretch, Iggy and I could look down on the tops of tall trees on each side. No wonder the Iron Range and Huron Bay Railroad failed! The story is that, on the test run, the one-hundred-ton locomotive tried to make it up the steep incline from the big ore docks at Huron Bay, fell off the track, and that was the end of the dream. But the roadway, though overgrown with alders and trees still remained, and Iggy and I followed it all the way to the shore of Lake Superior. Only a few pilings showed where the ore docks had been constructed, so we walked the beach to the mouth of the Big Huron River and back. Again I felt the vastness and purity of that great lake; again I was washed clean of all my tiny troubles. The magic was still there.

Returning, we decided to follow the Slate River up to its source rather than retrace our footsteps. Near the unmanned fire tower at Arvon, we made a bit of a detour to see the old slate mines from which, in the 1870s and 1880s, much of the slate used on roofs and for schoolchildren's slates had come. The claim was that Arvon produced the best slate in the world. It was carried by ox team to the shore, loaded on a schooner for the Soo, and from there it was shipped all over our country. We found the mines and also the foundations of an old settlement near them that held many artifacts. Someone with a metal detector should explore that place. I found a cobalt blue bottle for my packsack, while Iggy put a sheet of slate in his.

The Slate River turned out to be one of the most scenic I've ever known. Only about ten or fifteen feet wide, it runs to the lake in a series of cascades and waterfalls. Under one of them we stripped and sat naked, letting the crystal-clear water pour sensuously over our heads and shoulders. Everyone should sit under a waterfall at least once in his life.

Walking up that river was a delight, and just before we came to the tall ridge that was the divide of land, we found its source in a circle of springs, ten or twenty of them, each contributing its tiny stream to the others until they became a small river. The setting was superb. Without underbrush, the tall maples and birch, widely separated from each other, gave the impression of a park. I've always intended to go back to the happy valley of the springs but never did, and now I know I never can. I suppose by now they've logged it off. If they have, don't tell me.

Lake Superior and Ore Boat

Heading for home, we climbed the high ridge and made our night fire under some tall hardwoods not far from the deep railroad cut. Weary, both of us fell asleep immediately. Then suddenly I awakened to find that Iggy had disappeared. At first I thought he had just gone after more firewood but when I called and he didn't answer I became concerned. Straining my eyes in the darkness, I saw something moving beyond the edge of the firelight and running over there, I found Iggy walking in his sleep with his eyes open but glazed. "Where is he? Where is he?" he mumbled. When I grabbed and shook him until he awakened our night fire was just a tiny spark in the dark. Needless to say, I didn't sleep much the rest of that long night nor the next night because it took us two days to get back to the cabin. I still shudder with the thought that, had Iggy wandered west rather than east, he would have fallen sixty feet down into that railroad cut.

And so my blissful summers passed during that tough decade. But always there came a time when I had to go back to a civilization that had no place for a man with a tangled tongue, except at the cost of constant anxiety and frustration. Leaving the old cabin was always agony.

Waterfalls - Slate River

Hermit No More

By the end of that decade I started to conquer my stuttering, thanks mainly to an old man in a Model-T Ford on the road from Rhinelander, Wisconsin. I had taught that year at Saline and by spring I was in bad shape. I'd tried again to commit suicide. I'd become hooked on the barbiturates I'd taken from my father's dispensary and had undergone the trauma of cold turkey withdrawal. Though somehow I had managed to complete the school year, it was clear that I had to find a job that would involve little speaking. I found it.

On my way home from Saline, I took a bus to Chicago and Milwaukee and Wausau where it went west to Minneapolis, and there I started hitchhiking for home. Passing the driveway of a large dairy farm, I saw a hand-lettered sign that said "Help Wanted." Fearing instant rejection if I stuttered so grotesquely, I got out a pad and pencil and wrote: "I'm deaf and dumb but I'm a good worker and need a job." After he read it the farmer wrote, "OK. $25 a month and room and food."

It was long dirty work from dawn to dusk. I cleaned the barns, shoveled manure, fed the cows and did a lot of other chores. I had to eat, not with the family, but in the shed by myself. I slept in the barn. The family talked about their dummy in my presence, thinking that I could not hear them. It was rough but I kept telling myself that if, because of my stuttering, I couldn't earn my daily bread except at the cost of sheer torture, I would just exist. I would lower my needs and aspirations to zero and try not to think or feel anything. I would just endure.

What I Hungered For

Playing deaf mute, I stuck it out for almost a month, then found myself one day going through the garbage cans hunting for scraps of newspaper I might read. I quit the next day and started walking northward, feeling pretty rotten. I couldn't die and I couldn't live. The hunger for the old cabin and my lakes drove my footsteps.

Then I had an experience which eventually changed my life, gave me fluency, and helped me design a method for treating stuttering that has since spread over much of the world.

After I'd walked seven or eight miles, I became tired and was sitting under a tree to rest when along came an old man in a very old car. He stopped near me but hailed a farmer who was discing a field just behind my tree and they had a long conversation. I noted that the old man had an odd kind of speech full of little lags and stickings but thought nothing of it, being intent on asking him for a ride when he was finished. But he asked me first for which I was grateful and away we rattled. Then, of course, came the inevitable question: "What's yer name, Sonny, and where you going?" Oh, how I stuttered when I answered him. There were long blocks, head jerks, facial contortions, everything. When the old man began to laugh uproariously, I could have hit him but seeing my fury he said, "Now take it easy, Sonny. Take it easy! I'm not laughing at your stuttering. Hell, I'm a stutterer too, and I used to block and jump around like you do, but now I'm too old and tired to stutter so hard anymore. Just let the words leak out by themselves."

I can't describe the impact his words had on me. All my life I had tried to talk without stuttering and had used a thousand tricks to avoid or hide it. When I did stutter I fought and struggled to get my words out no matter what contortions ensued. That old man was telling me that it was possible to stutter so easily I could be fluent. It was a revelation. Don't try to talk without stuttering; change it to a brief, easy, fluent form of stuttering. I felt much as St. Paul must have felt on the road to Damascus.

I never forgot what that old man said to me, but I vowed I wouldn't wait until I was just too old and tired. I would learn his way or even a better way of stuttering easily. It proved to be harder than I thought. Indeed, it wasn't until 1931 when I went to the University of Iowa, where one of the first speech clinics had been created, that I mastered my unruly tongue and gained the ability to talk without contortions or fear, to stutter so easily and briefly that my impediment was almost unnoticeable.

Once I had accomplished this I felt consumed to try to help other stutterers to become free from their tangled tongues, so I entered a graduate program leading to a doctorate in clinical psychology, hoping to create my own speech clinic someday. At that time the field of speech pathology didn't exist and clinical psychology was the closest to it. Having a sparse background in psychology, I spent a year at the

University of Minnesota studying the subject, and then went back to Iowa to get my doctor's degree.

Because this is the tale of my U.P. lakes and forest and streams, I tell these things with some reluctance and do so only because my life up there changed drastically once I could talk. The old cabin, so silent after The Regulars stopped coming (even though I was in it) now came to life with laughter and conversation. Almost intoxicated by my new freedom to communicate, I needed others around me. No longer the wolf who walked by his wild lone, I needed companions to share with me the loveliness and joys of my beloved land.

So it was that for some years several of my friends from Tioga would visit me each weekend for a fish fry and hilarity. By this time the old wagon road was impassable, being so overgrown with tangles of alders that only a faint trail provided access. Because the loggers were not cutting pulp or the hardwoods up Wabeek Creek, I had cut that trail out of necessity. It crossed the river on a log above a swift rapids, then skirted across old beaver meadows, crossed the beaver dam creek to the place where the old wagon road climbed the big hill. From there on, the walking was easy.

Let me give one glimpse of one of those weekends with my friends. One afternoon, when I was just about out of grub and contemplating going to town for more, three of them arrived, Iggy, Mule Cardinal, and Reino Kangas. They brought blankets, fresh baked bread, newly churned butter and wild raspberry jam. To get our suppers we all went fishing immediately, catching enough bass and pike to fill two of the huge frying pans that The Regulars had used, and which still hang on the old cabin's walls.

To the White Boulder and Back

After cleaning the fish, to cleanse ourselves we swam naked all across the lake to the big white boulder, then back again. Peeling enough potatoes to fill the large kettle, we fried the fish outside over an open fire once the coals were right, but we ate the meal in the cabin and I think the old cabin sure enjoyed our noisiness. We laughed a lot and yelled a lot and drank our whiskey straight, young bucks out on a spree.

It seemed impossible that four young men could eat all that food but we did - all but about a third of the potatoes. Then Iggy made a proposition to Mule Cardinal. "Mule," he said, "if you can eat all the rest of those potatoes, I'll kiss your butt." Although, like all of us, he was bulging at the seams, Mule agreed. He ate and ate and ate those potatoes and we could see he was slowing down when his eyes were beginning to protrude. "Pass me the salt!" he ordered when only three potatoes were left. Gulping, he managed to get the first one down, then after a long pause the second. Mule stood up, took down his pants. "Well, Iggy," he said, "Get ready to pucker up." But he couldn't bite into that last potato. Groaning, he waddled over to the bottom bunk and crawled in as we hooted.

Mule didn't eat any breakfast that next morning, but he got his revenge that night when Iggy went first to bed and fell to sleep immediately with his mouth open and his hands supine on the blanket. When I saw that Mule had a dead mouse we'd caught and was about to put it in Iggy's open mouth I shook my head. "Put it in his open hand," I whispered. It looked kind of nice there curled in Igg's hand, but he didn't move. Indeed I was asleep when "Yeeow!" rent the silence. Iggy had found the mouse! We laughed so hard we couldn't get back to sleep, so we went outside and I led that crazy crew all over the clearing doing my Grampa Gage's Dance of the Wild Cucumber and chanting its immortal refrain: "Oh Tweedle Dee and Tweedle Dum, All hail Immortal Nose and Thumb." Creaky old bones and all, I still do that dance when the moon is full as it was that night.

I had other companions too. One of them, George Egland, was a stutterer I'd met during my year at the University of Minnesota. Almost as crazy about the forest as I was, he spent several weeks each summer fishing and roaming the woods with me. A gay, zany spirit, always ready for an adventure, he loved to scale the face of the sheer granite cliffs, then roll down big stones crashing into the forest below, yelling "Sittin de Mai", a Norwegian howl of exultation. Once when he, Iggy and I were camping out after fishing the Wabeek up by the Boilers, he innocently asked me if I'd ever caught a rabbit on a flyrod. When I said no, he looked surprised, and in the middle of that night a hell of a commotion occurred. Something, probably a bear, went charging over me and Iggy as we lay by the fire under our blankets. Iggy just pulled the blanket over his head but I crawled out to see Eg playing a big rabbit all over that clearing with his flyrod. He'd seen it poking its head out of the underbrush, contrived a loop of fishline and snared it. Lord how that crazy Norsk howled in triumph as he wore that poor rabbit out, took off the noose and stuffed it back in its hole with a sermon of caution. Once, on the Third Lake where an osprey had its nest atop a tall pine stub, Eg climbed up a tall fir tree beside it to see what was in the nest, only to have the osprey flail him with its wings so hard he had to give up. Another time, at the Haysheds, both of us got drunk on sugar plums that had fermented after an early frost. I think it was Eg, too, who persuaded me to swim under water with him through the hole of a big beaver house that we'd widened, and to sit there in the dim light gnawing on a poplar twig. Lord, we stank for weeks of beaver musk. A zany wonderful companion, we sure had fun together in the wilderness.

Then there was Arnold Hilden, my college roommate at the University of Iowa. City born and bred, he'd been intrigued by my tales of the northwoods, so one summer he came up to the old cabin to be with me for a week. After the first hour or so, Arne was almost frantic. The deep silence of the forest devastated him. He trailed me like a little dog, afraid to be alone. He talked compulsively day and night, but finally the great peace of the wilderness came to him. When, one day, he cut down a three-inch maple sapling, sawed a chunk from it, and whittled out a potato masher, I knew he was all right. It took him a whole day, a happy day.

The first white woman, as she called herself, to walk our trails was my second cousin, Sally Bonine, who came to the cabin on her honeymoon. She loved it but her new husband, Clyde, did not. Too primitive for him! Making a little fire on the southeast shore of our lake, they let it get away from them and it roared up the hill and my brother Joe and I had a hell of a time containing it. They left the next day and I was glad to see them go.

The next woman to see our lakes was also on her honeymoon with Tom Hedetniemi, my roommate during my University of Michigan days. Tom had been a good friend during my high-school years, and his wife Siiri, also a Finn, loved the forest. For several years they spent a week of their vacation in the old cabin as their names carved above the door attest. Although I let them have it to themselves most of the time, I visited them often and was deeply impressed by their loving relationship. Happy as I was, it was clear that I was missing something very important. For the first time in my life I had thoughts of getting married someday. Married? That was crazy! I was having too much fun with the girls at the university. Why should I get tied down to a wife and perhaps children? No, nothing would run around my house but a sidewalk. I loved my freedom. Nevertheless, having witnessed the love that Tom and Siiri had for each other, the thought kept haunting me.

It even kept on haunting me while I was working on my doctorate at Iowa where I was having a wonderful time studying, doing research, and chasing girls. Seashore, Dean of the Graduate College, chose Arnold Hilden and me as guinea pigs in an experiment in graduate education. We would be given the freedom of the university, allowed to sit in any class we wished and be freed from all exams and term papers. At the end of two years, however, we would be subjected to five days of written and one day of oral tests over the fields of abnormal psychology, speech and psychiatry, and be expected to do an excellent dissertation. Nothing of the sort had ever been tried before but it was right up my alley. I studied terribly hard and played harder, often getting no more than three hours of sleep but I had immense energies, probably due to my new ability to communicate. I felt as though I were a coiled spring that had suddenly been released. The world was my oyster to shuck and consume. Sometimes I overdid it, such as the time after a Homecoming football game when a policeman came upon me walking down the middle of Iowa Avenue at 3 A.M. holding a flashlight.

"Who are you, son, and what are you doing?" he demanded.

"I'm Diogenes," I replied, "and I'm looking for an honest man."

"You've found him," said the cop. "Come with me!" and so I spent the night in jail. Perhaps it is evidence of my essentially dissolute character but I've always been a bit proud of the experience. Everyone should spend one night in jail.

Old Cabin in Autumn

The old cabin even played an important role in helping me get my Ph.D. In preparing for those terrible exams I compiled three hundred cards, on each of which I wrote a topic or question on which I might be quizzed, then studied hard to acquire the information. That summer, each morning I would shuffle the cards, pick one, then give a lecture on the topic that had to last at least ten minutes without pausing. I set a quota of ten cards that I had to lecture on successfully or I wouldn't be able to go fishing or exploring in the afternoon. Because I had never spoken continuously in my life because of my stuttering, nor ever had to think on my feet, there were many days at first when I did no fishing, but I persevered and drove myself and finally did well. In later years I have often been grateful for the experience when I had to speak extemporaneously to large audiences, or to be interviewed on radio or TV. Yes, I owe a lot to the old cabin, and it knows more about psychoanalysis and hypnosis and a lot of other subjects than any other shack in the U.P.

Marriage

Finally tiring of woman-chasing and remembering Tom and Siiri, I hungered for a less transient relationship because I didn't want to spend the rest of my life alone. There was one girl, a very pretty girl, who liked me a lot and when she came to visit me one weekend in Iowa I almost thought I was in love with her. To make sure that the girl I married would love the U.P. as I did, I invited her to come to Tioga and my lakes. It was a disaster! She came with a suitcase full of frilly dresses and in high heels. She wouldn't try to walk the log over the rapids but sidled her way across it inch by inch. She hated the trail, complaining she thought it would never end. When she saw my beloved cabin she exclaimed, "Don't tell me you live in that miserable shack." Tom and Siiri, who were staying at the cabin and chaperoning, were very polite but it was obvious they didn't approve. She couldn't paddle the canoe, nor did she want to. The forest terrified her. That night a single mosquito kept her from sleeping, and when a porkie raised hell on the roof she kept screaming and crying long after Tom and I had chased the critter away. I took her back to town the next day, put her on the train, and that was that!

The next girl to bump her head on the door frame of the old cabin was Catharine Jane Hull whom I'd known during the year at Minnesota, when I was getting a background in psychology. Very attractive with brown eyes and lovely legs, she was also extremely intelligent, a Phi Beta Kappa like me.. I guess the reason she intrigued me at first was that she was always so poised, serene and composed. I wanted to muss her hair and find the gypsy I suspected lay behind that facade. At first she wasn't particularly interested in me but I teased her, bedevilled her, and wooed her in a hundred unexpected ways, including writing a sonnet to her big toe. All of her previous boyfriends had adored her and put her on a pedestal. I shook that pedestal and she liked it.

Also, as an instructor in the University of Minnesota's new speech clinic, she found me valuable in providing insights and suggestions for the stutterers with whom she did therapy. Almost every week we had dates together, going to symphonies, ice boating, plays, and even to church where I could hold her hand under the hymn book. And we talked and talked, for I found that watching her fine mind at work was almost as good as looking at her legs. By the end of that school year both of us were almost in love. I know that there were times when after leaving her I walked back to my rooming house with my head banging against the stars. When the school year ended I actually hated to go back to the old cabin. I couldn't bear living without her.

The following year when I was at the University of Iowa, three hundred miles away, both of us tried to keep the romance going, writing each other and phoning weekly. Twice she came down to go to her home in Washington, Iowa (The Cleanest Little City in Iowa, the sign said) and I managed to see her then and hold her in my arms at a dance. But absence makes the heart grow fonder - for somebody else - and by the end of the year I thought I'd lost her. Her replies to my letters were long delayed. When I phoned, she either wasn't there or sounded impatient. I heard she was dating a piccolo player in the Minneapolis Symphony Orchestra. Gad! So to hell with her! There were plenty of other girls, and when I got up to the old cabin it didn't seem to matter so much. Or so I told myself to dampen the ache.

Two years later, after I got my doctorate, and had taken off my cap and gown, I was deeply depressed. It was the height of the Great Depression and there were no jobs for clinical psychologists anywhere. What to do? At that moment there was a knock on the door and a special delivery letter from Catharine Jane Hull congratulating me on getting my degree. It was full of wonderful memories of the good times we'd had together. She said she missed me and thought of me often. There was affection in each sentence and it ended with "Yours, Katy." The next day I threw all my possessions in my old car and that night I held her in my arms again.

While there, I accepted an offer from Dr. Bryngelson, head of the University of Minnesota Speech Clinic, to operate a private clinic for stutterers for six weeks that summer. He'd rented a fraternity house and hired a house mother and cook. I could try out the new stuttering therapy I'd been experimenting with at Iowa. Did I want it? I sure did and I sure wooed Catharine Jane Hull that summer. This time the romance lasted, probably because I'd wangled a postdoctoral fellowship to investigate the causes of stuttering, and it gave me a car and per diem expenses because we had advertised over the radio and in the newspapers to locate children who had just begun to stutter. Since my job was to interview and test the beginning stutterers and their parents, I travelled all over Iowa for two years on that research program, managing my itinerary so I could get to see Katy as often as possible.

The next summer, my mother wrote her mother suggesting that Katy visit us in Tioga, saying that she thought her son was very much in love with Mrs. Hull's daughter. That's how they did it back then, formal as hell. When I found out she had written I was delighted, but afraid that Katy might refuse and even more afraid, remembering the fiasco with the other girl, that she might accept the invitation. But she came!

Ready for the forest even before she got off the train, Katy was dressed in jodhpurs and boots when I met her at 5:30 in the morning. Because my family was still in bed, I drove her up to an especially lovely spot on the Tioga and we had coffee and cookies over a little fire. When we returned to my home, within minutes she had charmed all of my family completely, even my father by asking him good questions about the baby case he'd been on the night before. Her father was a country doctor too. Shortly afterward, my mother took me aside. "Cully," she said, "if you don't marry that delightful young woman you'll break my heart."

But I had to make sure. So we spent a night and two days up at the old cabin and lakes with Tom and Siiri as chaperones. They too liked her immediately. Crossing that log over the roaring rapids, she was petrified but when I told her the other girl had sidled across it on her bottom, Katy tossed her head and walked across it with big steps. She loved the forest trail, the tall ferns, even the steep hill she had to climb. Although she bumped her head entering, I could tell she was fascinated by the old cabin.

To a girl from the farmlands of Iowa and the noise of Minneapolis, everything was strange and intriguing. I took her along the Upper Lake trail to the great rocks of Porcupine Bluff, through the giant hardwoods and the long birch hill to the big spring. After she pressed her face to the icy water and drank she said, "Oh, Cully, now I understand why you love this place so much." That evening we went out in the canoe to hear the night sounds and again she was enthralled, and I discovered she could paddle a canoe like an expert.

After a regrettably virginal night I awakened to find her gone. She was down on my favorite log at the edge of the lake watching the swirling fog devils rising from the east bay. Later, when I took her to the second lake, she was entranced by its beauty. "Why, it's just like one of those mountain lakes I saw when I visited the Rockies," she exclaimed. Indeed it does look like one, surrounded as it is with cliffs, then disappearing around the furthermost hills. All my doubts vanished. She was the one! I was so happy I could hardly bear it and when she left on the train I could hardly fish. Lord, I had it bad! I sure was in love with Catharine Jane Hull.

Two years later we were back at the old cabin again - this time on our honeymoon. I'd finally found a job, one that I really wanted. It was to create a speech clinic at Western Michigan Teachers College in Kalamazoo. I would be paid the munificent sum of $3000 a year, which was a lot back then, and I would have my summers off. Oho! Right up my alley! Driving directly to Minneapolis, I proposed. In later years my wife insisted that I did so on bended knee, which is hard to believe, but anyway she said yes. Knowing that she had always hoped to honeymoon at Lake Louise in Banff, I told her I thought I had enough money to manage it, but to my great delight and relief, she said no, that she'd prefer to go to the old cabin in the forest.

When we got there we found that my so-called friends had been there before us. The perfect balsam bed in the upper bunk that I had prepared so carefully before I went to Iowa to get married was heaped high with logs. The dirty buggers! I was able to get all but one of them outside but that one, a big spruce log, was wedged in so tightly I couldn't budge it. I could almost hear the old cabin laughing as we spent that night in twin beds, and it took me all the next morning to get the log out of there.

Second Lake

While I was working on it, Milady Katy was busy cleaning house, even sweeping many years of cobwebs off the log walls. Then, prowling the forest, she returned draped in strings of ground pine, the lovely vine with little green spikes that grows so lushly in our hardwoods. These she fashioned into curtains for the three windows and with the table set for two and with three candles nested in Indian slates, the old cabin had never looked better. Our home in the forest.

After supper, we paddled the canoe all around the lake, listening to the night sounds. "What was that?" "Oh, that's a partridge drumming on a hollow log wanting to make love. A red squirrel wound itself up and let its ratchet go as a deer came down to the shore to drink.

Gaboom! Gaboom! That's one of the very large bullfrogs we see around here occasionally. The millionaire, Cyrus McCormick, loved to eat frog legs and so he imported and planted them in White Deer Lake where he had his big lodge. From there they escaped and spread widely. Once at the Wigwam near the source of the Big Huron, one of them sounded off and Mullu, my companion, told me it was a cow beaver calling her young."

Inside the Old Cabin

Over by the spring a fox barked and a pileated woodpecker shattered the silence hammering on a dead cedar. Whippoorwills sounded the call that gave them their name. An owl by Birch Point kept inquiring who we were with its "Who-Who?" There's a spot on the lake by Pine Point where once I heard seven echoes from the hills, in response to my shouting the old riverman's call of "Ai-yee." When we paddled over there and I invited my bride to see how many echoes she could evoke, she refused. "No, Cully," she said. "I just can't do it. Why profane the night?" I could have hugged her but you just can't do that in a canoe.

The night got profaned anyway. After we were asleep in each other's arms a terrible commotion occurred outside. Someone was beating on the corrugated steel sheets of the roof; men were yelling and shouting; all hell had broken loose. "Chivari!" they hollered, "Chivaree! Booze and money! Chivaree!" Katy pulled the blankets over her head as I climbed down to light a candle. In they came, six or seven young men, full of the devil. I recognized Mullu and Fisheye and Iggy but the others were strangers. When I brought out the only bottle of whiskey I'd lugged up in my packsack they drank it all, passing the bottle around. Chivaree!

Chivaree

How in the world they'd been able to cross that log and come up the faint trail in the black night I don't know. Certainly the two kerosene farm lanterns they carried couldn't have provided much light. But there they were yelling and laughing and giving me lewd advice on how to get the job done. Nevertheless, it was a tribute of sorts and an old U.P. custom, so I couldn't help laughing with them. Finally, after about an hour they left, giving the roof a good walloping as they departed.

Crawling up into the top bunk, I tried to explain. We were now officially married, I told Milove. It wouldn't happen again. There was only one chivaree to a marriage and I intended to stay married to her for a long, long time. Still shocked and weeping a little, all she could say was, "Take me back to Iowa." Just before I closed my eyes I thought I saw the logs at the bottom of the bunk grinning.

For the three weeks of that honeymoon it rained every day though not all day every day and we certainly got acquainted. Katy liked her pancakes thick; I wanted mine thin. She wanted her oatmeal soupy; I wanted mine granular. Her meat had to be rare; mine well done. It didn't matter ; we were very much in love.

For the first time the old cabin was full of flowers: daisies, Indian paintbrush, and especially blue gentians, her favorite. It was full of good cooking smells too. Having picked a hatful of blueberries from Hedet Point, she baked a fine pie in the cranky old wood range, rolling out the crust with an empty whiskey bottle. The pie was burned a bit on one edge but it was certainly a lot better than the one I'd baked years before, when what I thought was flour turned out to be woodfiber plaster. How I enjoyed seeing Katy move around the old cabin, doing little dance steps and singing the old songs such as "Heart of My

Heart." When I wasn't hugging her, I was hugging myself. How could I have been so lucky?

Several afternoons when the sun did come out, the two of us went down to the sandy beach to swim naked and frolic around. Like little children we played on the sand, making castles and canals.

One morning she caught a very large bass which I estimated to be about six pounds, a really big one. Katy had seen the smoked head of the seven pounder I'd caught years before and she wanted me to smoke this one. Unfortunately, I didn't tend the fire as well as I should have done and its big head shriveled to a very small one. Furious, she gave me blue fits, accusing me of doing it on purpose. Once when I left her alone in the cabin to get her some trout from Wabeek Creek, I didn't get back until long after dark and found her in very angry tears. Yes, during that honeymoon I found the gypsy in her. The three weeks passed by very swiftly and when it was time to go, she tapped the logs of the old cabin saying, "We'll be back, old cabin. We'll be back." Every year until she died she said the same farewell.

Our Third Lake

That fall the hunger to go deer hunting grabbed me. For ten years, with college and teaching, I'd been unable to do so. It really wasn't the hunting that drew me north; I just wanted to see the forest, lakes and streams in their winter dress, to see again the white wonderland I remembered. But did I dare ask for the time off? After all, I'd just been on the job for two months.

However, I'd heard that Dr. Sangren, president of the college, always went deer hunting, so with some trepidation I asked him if I could go. "Go deer hunting?" Of course, you can go deer hunting. Why do you think I've stayed in Michigan these years? Just get someone -

67

even if it's the janitor - to take your classes." Whoops! I told him my wife had taught the subjects at the University of Minnesota and was very competent.

So, in 1936, I had ten blissful days up at the old cabin in November, with my father as a hunting companion. The first day the lake froze over and I watched, fascinated, to see it happen. Beginning at the shoreline, little slivers of ice would project themselves into the lake, then the water between them would freeze. Then a large pane of ice would suddenly congeal in an instant. Within just an hour the east bay was covered and the next morning the whole lake was a still sheet of white snow. Sorcery! St. Urho, the Finn God of Snow, had waved his wand.

For two days it snowed quietly. Large flakes of snow drifted down lazily but constantly. There was no wind. The woods were absolutely still. Not even the clatter of a red squirrel spoiled the utter silence. Tilting my face to become one with the heavily-laden balsams and spruce, I soon became the abominable snowman walking quietly through the forest. When I got to the cabin I had to reach in for the broom before I looked human.

I've always felt sorry for the people from Down Below who, because they've toured it in the summer, think that they have seen the beauty of the Upper Peninsula of Michigan. In winter it's a totally different place and, in my opinion, much more beautiful. The myriad contours of the snow, each with its own odd shadows, the fir trees shaggy with their white burden, the hemlocks with their silver crowns are wonderful to behold. To walk through the winter woods seeing the maple saplings standing to attention, the fallen logs covered with polar bear rugs, the black shadows of tree branches on the untouched carpet of white, all these and a thousand other sights can only be known in winter time. I sure felt privileged to be there that deer season.

When the snow stopped, Dad and I had a day of heavy wind with the temperature near zero. Going down the hill trail to chop a hole for water I saw what seemed like frozen waves on the sand beach, a vista of corrugated snow. With the wind, the spruce and balsam trees were shrugging off their mantles and lifting their arms again to the sky. Several of them also shed a bucketful down my neck. The pines moaned and sliver cats groaned. (Sliver cats are leaning trees that rub against one another.) Branches cracked as they broke. The forest was full of sound.

The old cabin's roof was covered with white except where the chimney pipes pierced the roof, and it also wore a fringe of long white and blue icicles that we would use for our whiskey that evening. Unlike the day before when the chimney smoke rose straight up in a tall blue-white column , it was now a twisted grey wreath.

Entering the old cabin, I felt again its warmth and comfort, almost as though I were a babe in mother's arms. I put on some Habitant pea soup to simmer on the chance that Dad might come back for lunch, though he rarely did so. Usually he'd be out hunting from dawn to dusk, but that day the wind was terribly strong. Taking my rifle, I walked south to the beaver dam without seeing a single deer track, and when I returned I found my father hanging his red mackinaw on the bar above the box stove. "Not a fit day for man nor beast," he said. "The deer aren't moving. They're holed up under a windfall in the swamps. I went to the east end of the escarpment and saw no sign at all." He enjoyed the pea soup, then took a long nap. After doing the dishes, I sat in the big Morris chair for a long time thinking how good it was to be up there with him. For the first time he seemed to have recognized that I was a man, not a boy.

Winter Scene

That evening when I went down to get some morning water, the wind had ceased and millions of stars covered the dark sky. Once again I marvelled at how bright they were compared to how they looked Down Below. Across the lake the Big Dipper pointed the way to Lake Superior as a big red star (Betelgeuse) sat on a pine tree. "I think it's getting a lot warmer," I told my father when I put down the water pail. "The wind has died. I'll bet the deer will run tonight."

Old Cabin In Snow

He nodded. "Yes, we'll see tracks tomorrow. How thick is the ice on the lake?"

When I told him it was less than half an inch thick, he said that more was needed if we had to drag a deer on it, that you needed at least a full inch. Then he told me a long tale about how Toutloff had shot a big deer where the stream from the third lake enters our big one. "The ice seemed thick enough," he said, "but it wasn't. All four of us kept close to shore as we took turns dragging it but just this side of the rocky point all of us broke through, all at the same time. Fortunately the water there was only three feet deep. Good thing it hadn't happened as we rounded the point, where the water is fifteen feet deep."

I asked him if they'd stayed on the ice after they got out. "Oh no," he replied. "One dip in that ice water was enough. We hauled it up to the lake trail through the brush and brought it back that way. It was hard walking because our pants were frozen solid and it took us almost a night and a day to thaw out."

Dad was in his storytelling mood. Lighting his curved pipe and gesturing with it for emphasis, or lighting it again for suspense, he told of all the deer he had shot over the years. The detail was incredible. He remembered where they were, how they looked, how he aimed, everything. And once again he told of Old Napoleon whom he'd pursued all his days in vain. Finally, when Dad dozed off in the middle of a sentence, I loaded the box stove with green wood and it was time to crawl into our bunks.

It seemed as though I'd hardly closed my eyes when Dad let out the old lumberjack wake-up call, "Daylight in the swamp! Roll out!" It was five-thirty, he said, time to get going. Stumbling out of the lower bunk beneath him, I lit the lamp, put dry wood on the box stove's coals, made

70

a fire in the range, cut slices of bacon from the slab and mixed the pancake batter. Almost an hour later when the cabin was very warm, Dad arose, looking comical as he put on his red hunting cap to go outside. And patriotic too, with his long white nightshirt and the blue bed socks my mother had knitted for him! When he returned he said that it had thawed all night, that we'd see lots of tracks and that he'd get Old Napoleon for sure.

After the hearty breakfast it was still dark as tar outside but Dad was raring to go. "It'll be half an hour before I can see to shoot," he said, "but I'll sit on that flat rock at Porcupine Bluff until daylight comes. Then I'll take the lake trail west, just moseying along, and hike to the end of the second lake. If I'm not back by four-thirty, come after me with the lantern. My tracks will stay fresh today." Making himself a sandwich and grabbing a flashlight, he tucked his rifle under his arm and left. He sure had the fever and I prayed he wouldn't shoot a buck way over there. Lord, it would take me a day to drag it back.

After doing the dishes and putting out two pancakes for the whiskey jacks (the Canadian jays), I went down to the lake for more water and to see the sun come up. The water hole was open and the air was balmy. It would be a fine day.

It was! Even before noon the temperature was over forty. Under a sunny cloudless sky, walking was a real pleasure in the melting snow, although I slipped when going up a hill. Deer tracks were everywhere, the first one appearing within sight of the cabin. The delicate tracery of mouse tracks showed where one had emerged from a round hole, danced around, then reentered it again. A partridge had left a trail of webbed footprints by some cedars, and it startled me by flushing even as I examined them. Wishing I'd left my red hunting coat back at the cabin because it was so warm, I took it off and carried it over my left arm knowing it was a dumb thing to do if any deer happened to come by. But it was spring! Spring! Unbelievable spring! Little rivulets coursed down the black rocks on the south side of the hills. The west bark of trees had lost the snow plaster that had built up there just the day before; the twigs no longer had their white fur but now glistened wet in the sunshine; big chunks of snow kept falling from the firs. Oh, it was good to be alive and in the U.P. on such a day.

That afternoon after lunch I reminded myself I was there to hunt deer, so I took a long rounder around the south side of the beaver pond, then northward back to the lake, jumping two deer but not getting a shot. At the head of the swamp near a heavy deer trail I was leaning against a tree when a doe and fawn passed not forty feet away. I know they saw me because the doe's ears twitched and it stopped, but after looking at me for a long time they went their way. How graceful they were! Why would anyone want to shoot a deer?

Then suddenly I heard a loud Kaboom. The shot was so loud and seemed so near I almost ducked. It was Dad's rifle for sure. I waited for the finishing shot but it didn't come. Hurrying toward the lake I cut across Dad's trail going back toward the cabin and, following it, I found him field dressing a fine buck. "One shot!" Dad said triumphantly. "Dropped him in his tracks. Never knew what hit him." After he'd finished cleaning it, I gave him my gun and dragged the deer back to camp. It was so easy going in the wet snow, I only had to rest once.

My Father

As he helped me hoist the buck onto the pole, Dad kidded me a little. "Tomorrow I'll shoot a buck for you and then we'll go home," he said. "Trouble with you, Cully, is that you're always enjoying the scenery and not hunting hard enough. You've got to learn to concentrate every minute."

There's an old U.P. saying that if you don't like the weather, wait a day. Well, I liked that weather very much but the next day it was gone. We awoke to an entirely different world. During the night it had frozen so hard you could walk on the crust though you crunched with every step and the snow squeaked underfoot. A pale sun shone brightly but there was no warmth in it. It was very, very cold. Nevertheless, the forest was even more beautiful because every branch, every twig was encased in glittering ice. A fairyland of glass, I again found it difficult to concentrate on hunting.

I was in the cedar swamp back of the northeast bay that afternoon when I got my deer. Sitting on a log, I had just lit my pipe when I heard it coming. Crunch! Crunch! It too was breaking through the crust. Holding my breath, I waited for it to come into view. For a moment I had a brief glimpse of a gray ghostly shape making its way through the thick tangle, then it disappeared though I could still hear the deer approaching. Then the crunching suddenly stopped. Straining my eyes, I saw the back end of a deer behind some thick trees, then something that looked like its head. But were there antlers? We Gages don't shoot does. Yes, I thought I saw some but were they horns or tree branches? If only it would move! Very, very slowly I shifted position and was convinced. The head, my target, seemed very small in my rifle sights when I squeezed the trigger but down the deer dropped. When I got to it, I was appalled. Where were the big antlers I had seen? God help me, I'd shot a doe! Sick to my stomach, I looked more closely. No, it was a buck, a spikehorn, but were those horns long enough? They had to be at least three inches long to be legal game. Without a ruler, I couldn't be sure but they seemed to be pretty close. When Dad first saw it he was upset but he too thought the spikes might be long enough, just barely.

So we broke camp the next day and went home. By pressing a ruler tight against the skull, I found that one prong was three and a quarter inches long and the other exactly three. To ship the deer by train I had to get a permit from a game warden. He too lifted his eyebrows when he first saw the horns and measured them very carefully. "OK," he said, "but you must have been damned close!"

I will not belabor these pages with more stories of deer hunting. Suffice it to say that every November for fifty years has found me roaming the forest with my rifle under my arm. For the first thirty of those years I got my buck almost every season but thereafter only occasionally, mainly because there aren't as many deer as there were back then and perhaps because I haven't wanted to shoot another. The last one I shot I sure regretted. In dragging it back to camp, every step was a penance. Just walking in the winter woods is enough, that and the companionship and man talk by the fire.

In his seventies and eighties my father and some of my friends provided that fellowship. Dad was like a man possessed, hunting hard from daylight to dark but he was after only one quarry, Old Napoleon, and refused to shoot any other deer.* Once he did shoot a monster buck weighing over 200 pounds but when he saw it he said, no, that wasn't Old Napoleon. Too small! I broke two ribs hauling that huge deer in to camp and it was hard to breathe for a month. But it was always fun to be at the old cabin in November.

That summer of 1937 I didn't have to teach so Katy and I, after going to Iowa and Minneapolis for auld lang syne, went north to Duluth, then followed the shoreline of Lake Superior eastward through Wisconsin to the U.P. We collected agates by Ontonagon, spent a night in our sleeping bags in the Porcupine Mountains, and made our way through the old copper mining towns to Fort Wilkins at the top of the Keweenaw Peninsula. I wanted her to see more of my beloved land than that just around our lakes. Retracing our route,southward, we took a side trip to Skanee so I could share with her the waterfalls of the Slate River. While I made her a balsam bed, she caught four brook trout for our supper under a little waterfall not ten feet from our fire. Katy slept very well all night but I didn't because a damned bear kept snuffling around in the brush until dawn. When my wife asked me why my eyes were so red next morning, I told her only that I'd kept putting new wood on the fire all night.

That long summer was an utter delight with blissful days and even better nights. One highlight was the privilege to study two loons as they nested behind Birch Point, laid their eggs and hatched two babies. Being careful not to disturb them, we'd paddle the canoe across the lake, then walk quietly through the birches to a glade where we could watch them day after day. We even saw one of the loonlings break open its speckled olive-brown shell and emerge in a wet ball of fluff. And we watched the young loons learn how to swim, how to dive, and how to hitch rides on their mother's back.

How we enjoyed listening to those loons. To some, they seem to be laughing maniacally as they take off from the surface, but to us their wild tremolo seemed more a yell of triumph for becoming airborne. They are large heavy birds and getting off the water takes some doing. The Chippewa Indian name for them means "Walk-on-Water" but they don't walk; they run, leaving a wake behind them. That tremolo is also sounded when, as if in play, they dip, plunge, stand on their tails, then do it again and again just for the hell of it. "Look at me! See what I can do!" they seem to say. Often they join each other in a duet. To hear that impetuous tremolo is to hear the essence of the wilderness.

*I have a tale about Dad's last encounter with Old Napoleon in my first Northwoods Reader.

Lake of the Clouds: Porcupine Mountains

But loons have another sound too, the wail, that echoes from the hills, especially at evening as dusk approaches. Often it almost sounds like a wolf howl except that the latter rises and falls, whereas the wail of the loon goes up and just hangs there quivering. Often another loon will answer and once we heard a quartette when loons from another lake joined those in ours.

Nesting Loon

Then there is another sound they make which few have heard, a blend of chirp, chuckle and quack. Very soft, the only time we heard it was when the mother loon was teaching her babies to dive. By that time the loonlings were about five inches long, and able to swim very well as they tagged along after the adult. The mother (or father; it's hard to tell) would lead them out from shore, then suddenly dive. When she disappeared, the two little ones would swim close to each other until the mother surfaced near them. Over and over again the mother did this until finally one of the babies got the idea and dived too. The other baby looked pretty disconsolate to us and it was a slow learner. Indeed it wasn't until the mother swam over it and ducked it under that it finally achieved the skill. We spent many hours watching those loons.

The other highpoint of that idyllic summer that I recall clearly was an afternoon that we spent on the second lake. It was one of those glorious U.P. days, all blue sky and sunshine. We poled the canoe down my tortuous canal between the two lakes, then explored every inch of the shoreline, even hiking down the outlet stream to the Tioga. I showed her the sheer bluff from which in my folly I'd jumped in a messy dive, landing on my back. We lingered a long time in the middle of a huge patch of white water lilies in the northwest bay, then paddled back to the big rocks. There in the moss and under the ferns we made love. Afterwards she lazily asked me to promise that someday I would build her a cabin on that very spot. Lord, at that moment I would have promised her the moon, so of course I said yes, knowing full well that it would be impossible. There were no roads within miles; building a cabin there was out of the question. "It's not that I don't love the old cabin," she said, "but someday we'll have children and grandchildren and will need more room. This is our special place, Cully." Little did I realize that her impossible dream would someday come true.

To have my wife know more about the beauty of the Upper Peninsula we drove home very slowly, making many little side trips to places I had known and treasured. We took a launch to see the Pictured Rocks at Munising, but the only picture we could imagine was that of an Indian in a blurred canoe. After the interminably long Seney stretch, we turned north to the quaint little fishing village of Grand Marais and spent a wonderful night sleeping on the Grand Sable Dunes. Again I felt the immensity and purity of the great lake and Katy did too, because just before we put out our evening fire she hugged me hard and said, "Two specks and a spark; that's all we are."

The Tahquamenon Falls were unforgettable and awe inspiring. We watched them a long time. Then on we drove to the Soo where we watched ships going through the locks and saw the great rapids of the St. Marys River, down which in the old days the Indians precariously ran their canoes, scooping up whitefish with hand nets. Then to the ferry. All in all we covered much of the upper part of the U.P., and I was happy to find that Katy loved every inch of it too. What a beautiful land!

The next summer, in 1938, I accepted an offer to be a visiting professor at the University of Minnesota for the months of June and July, administering their new speech clinic and teaching two classes. I enjoyed the job but begrudged the time away from the old cabin, though we did manage to spend all of August in it. The most important thing that happened that summer, however, occurred in bed and, as the old U.P. saying goes, "It sure changed the water on the minnows." We were in each other's arms one night when Katy said, "I want a baby, Cully." I agreed. "Yes" I said, "in two or three years we ought to start having a family. "No!" she replied. "Right now!" I jumped out of bed and spent the night on the couch in the living room. And the next and the next before I gave in. I didn't want any little rivals; I wanted all her affection.

Tahquamenon Falls

Fatherhood

The next year in June our first child, Cathy, was born, then two years later Sue arrived, and in two more I had a son, John. Most of them were conceived in the old cabin or in special nesting spots around our lakes. Having the babies so close together meant that Katy was often unable to be with me when I returned to the lakes for a week or two each summer, except for a night or two. She and the babies stayed in town at my father's house, and so did I. Somehow the magic of living alone up there had vanished. Wandering the forest and fishing the lakes and streams was not enough now. Missing my wife and children too much when I was away from them, I couldn't wait till they were old enough to join me.

Our first child to enter the old cabin was Cathy. Only three years old at the time, she insisted on walking the whole way, even refusing to be carried up the steep hill. By this time some loggers were cutting pulp up at the headwaters of the Wabeek, had opened up the old wagon road, and had built a bridge across the river. We were able then to park the car there but it was still a long hike for a little girl. I can still see Cathy's little blonde head bobbing through the tall ferns as the path wound along the base of the granite cliffs. Carrying a tiny packsack containing one roll of toilet paper, she was very tired when at last we reached our destination. "Hello, old cabin, I'm Cathy," she said, then crawling into the lower bunk she promptly fell sound asleep but not before saying, "My bed in the woods." A great sense of fulfillment swept over me. All this and heaven too!

I had the same feeling the next morning when, with Cathy sitting in the middle of the canoe, Katy and I paddled over to the big spring. I made her a little birch bark cup from which she drank in delight, then used it to help me fill the old brown jug. Meanwhile her mother was weaving a tiara of cedar sprigs, no, two of them, one for the little blonde head and the other for her own bonny brown hair. Queens of the Lake! I sure felt blessed. Two queens and a jack; better than a royal flush!

A few years later when our children were one, three and five, all of us spent several days at the old cabin. John rode in the packsack with the grub and wailed all the way, but we had a fine time after we got there, even with all five of us in the canoe. One dark night I put John again in the packsack and by flashlight carried him through the dark woods to the hill overlooking the beaver dam where we sat on a log for a bit. Imprinting! Today he doesn't remember the experience of course, but he loves the forest almost as much as I do.

Milady Katy and Cathy

While many of my recollections have faded, I do recall a wonderful week when the three children were four, six and eight. Leaving the car by the bridge, I led my little troop up the trail, so happy I almost burst. It was a very good week. Each morning the children collected treasures to show us: a red mushroom, a salamander, a perfect circle of green moss, a frond of maidenhair fern, an empty clam shell, that sort of thing. Cathy found the base of a Canadian thistle with its petals symmetrically arranged around the stem, and insisted on using it as a plate for her lunch. John found a shiny black beetle that ferociously snapped its tiny jaws. Sue drew a picture of the cabin on an Indian slate. Yes, being a father was very good. Not only did I still have my wife's affection but that of my children too. To lift them high in my arms and then to have them hug me on the way down saying, "I love you, Daddy-o" is a memory I treasure. Up there at the old cabin we became very close.

I always took each of the children in turn for a short canoe ride each day. Cathy said nothing, just watched the trees and the swirling water and the waves; Sue talked all the time; John kept wanting to fish. So I rigged up a rod with a bobber and worm and let him catch some of the little bass that were always by the deadhead and he's been hooked on fishing ever since. Once John caught a four-pound bass and, cranking furiously, had it flopping from the end of the rod before I got to him to help him land it. That at the age of four!

Of all our children, John was the only one we worried about up there in the forest. Cathy, our animal person, could be left alone playing with a toad or chipmunk for hours. Susan was always with one of us talking and asking questions we found hard to answer, such as "Why is a spruce prickly and a balsam smooth?" But we had to watch John every moment. He was a roamer and explorer, completely unafraid of anything. Once, when I was fishing by Herman's Rock I heard his mother calling him and then me with great urgency. I've never paddled a canoe so fast as I did then. "John's lost," she cried. "I've called and called and he doesn't answer." I shared her anxiety. Up there in the big woods a little boy can get lost very easily.

I told the girls to go into the cabin and stay there, and my wife to go south calling him, while I went north, and if that failed we'd go east and west. Well, I soon found him not too far from the cabin. He was behind a huge moss-covered boulder trying to climb it. "Why didn't you answer when you heard us calling?" I demanded, giving him a little swat on the bottom. "Cause then you'd come after me," he replied very logically. So I hugged him hard, set him atop the big rock, called him "King of the Woods" and that was that. His sisters always called him "Bullet Head" but the term should have been bull, not bullet. John always has had a mind of his own.

In the afternoons all five of us would go down to the sandy beach to play nakedly on the sand and in the warm water, making harbors for our bark boats, spearing clams, frolicking in the little waves. Lazy, sweet afternoons in the sun, I wished that time could suddenly stop.

After supper we'd gather stuff for the evening fire we always had in the little clearing outside the cabin: birch bark, twigs, small wood. I also cut a big armful of dead spruce or balsam branches still covered with brown needles so we could take turns burning them after it got dark. When ablaze, these branches curl up into little fists of fire. The Finns call them "kuolema goru" which means "hands of death." When the kuolema goru were all burned up, the five of us would sit there by the dying fire, oh so close, listening to the night sounds or gazing up at the stars high in the branches of the great maples. John always sat between my legs and Cathy and Sue had a mother's arm around them. When the mystery of the night and the wilderness overcame them, suddenly the children would bolt for the safety of their bunks inside the cabin, giggling deliciously. With my arm around my wife and smoking the last pipe of the day, life was very, very, good.

At the end of the week when the grub was gone and it was time to leave, Katy made each of the kids tap the logs of the old cabin three times for "I love you" then say, "I'll be back, old cabin." Then she said it,

80

Sue, John and Cathy

and I said it, and down the trail we'd go. I can still hear their sweet high voices incongruously singing "Jingle Bells."

I think it was the summer after that when another halcyon week ended less favorably. First came the tap dancing of rain on the corrugated steel roof, then a chorus of pitter and patter, then the continuous roar of heavy rain. The big drops soaked me to the hide in minutes when I went outside. For two days it poured, while Katy and I did our best to keep the kids entertained and busy. I had John take a fishing reel apart, oil it and put it back together. Cathy wrote a story about horses, Susie drew more pictures, and we sang a lot. It was with great relief that we greeted the sun on the third day and started down the trail for the car.

As we approached the car, catastrophe! We found a raging, roaring flood with the bridge swept away. Even as we watched, the last long stringer broke loose and careened downstream. We were marooned! The car had been parked on the wrong side. I told Katy to take the kids back to the cabin and that I'd swim the river, hike to town, buy groceries, and have Dad bring me back. I'd return by dark. Katy told me later that Susie had cried all the way but the other two had held their heads high. All she had to feed them was one banana and a half box of oatmeal.

Well, I bought the groceries, including steaks for all, held them over my head as I swam one-handedly across the river, and got back to find the cabin candlelit and everyone content. In two days Finn loggers had put up a new bridge so we could pull out, but the experience had its effect on the two girls. For some years they were very reluctant to go with us up to the lakes. Though they did so to please us, they sure kept an eye on the weather. To John, it was just another good adventure.

Always on our trips to and from our lakes our family camped out along the way, exploring new places in the U.P. where we'd never been before, always finding new beauty. We slept in our sleeping bags by our night fire under a tarp, feeling our closeness and unity. Along the north shore of Lake Michigan we camped near that lovely little white church at Brevort, at the Big Spring west of Manistique, on the shore at Little Bay de Noc. One night in the sand dunes south of Gould City, a man carrying a rifle came into the firelight and gave me hell. "You ought not to be camping here," he said angrily. "There's a maverick sow bear with cubs just up the beach a short way who mauled another fool like you last week." No bear showed up, perhaps because I kept the fire going until four in the morning when a heavy downpour drenched us. We packed up and left, pouring John still in his sleeping bag into the back seat. He didn't wake up until we stopped for breakfast.

Kitchi-ti-ki-pi Springs near Manistique

Then there was the glorious afternoon and night that we slept on the shore of Lake Superior at Whitefish Point north of Paradise. The kids played and swam in the icy waters of the big lake until their lips turned blue and I had to stuff them into their sleeping bags to thaw until supper time. That night all of us were entranced as we watched the Northern Lights fanning spectacularly over the water.

Once we took a ferry-cruise ship from the Soo across to Thunder Bay in Canada. They had a luxurious dining room aboard ship and John drank out of the finger bowl. Because it was a night trip across that immense inland sea, I arose at dawn to see us passing Isle Royale. But what I remember best about that trip was the night we camped at the mouth of the Black River just east of the Wisconsin line. After supper John played in the wreck of an old fishing vessel that had washed ashore from Lake Superior. "When I'm old and have lots of money I'm going to buy this ship," he said, "and sail it right up to the old cabin." That night with my wife and the girls sleeping under the tarp and John in his pup tent, I was dozing by the fire when a mother skunk appeared, followed by three baby skunks, all in single file. I didn't move a muscle and hoped my family wouldn't either as the skunks climbed all over the sleeping bags before they finally left. Phew! I can well imagine what would have transpired had the kids awakened. Yes, Phew!

Shore of Lake Michigan

On still another expedition, starting from Iowa so we could show Katy's parents their grandchildren, we drove to Duluth, then all around the north shore of Lake Superior, through Wawa with its big statue of a wild goose, down to the Soo, and then to Tioga and our lakes. It was beautiful country too but no better than our wilderness lakes in the U.P. I've done a lot of traveling over the years but I've seen nothing better than my own little bit of the U.P. I confess my prejudice. I was imprinted early.

During their high school years, though our children came north with us every summer, they rarely came up to the old cabin. They were just having too much fun in Tioga, the girls with summer romances and John with his Finn and French Canadian friends. While they stayed at my father's home, Katy and I were often at the cabin with our own romance. We honeymooned all over again.

How swiftly those years flew by! Our children left home for college, then jobs, then marriages and children of their own. Rarely could they join us at the lakes when Katy and I went there every summer. In a way, it was probably just as well because the old cabin was disintegrating. The base logs were rotting; the door hung askew; the wood range was so rusted we could not use it. The roof leaked and there were wide spaces at the corners through which flies and mice came and went at will. So much brush had grown in the trail we had to look carefully to see it.

Whitefish Point

Then there came a year when, packing in our supplies, we found the old cabin completely uninhabitable. Someone had left the door ajar during the winter and the porcupines had wrecked the place. Their droppings were everywhere, even in the bunks. Tables, benches and chairs had been gnawed. Broken dishes and pots and pans were scattered all over the floor. Katy and I took one look and headed back to Tioga. Later, Joe and Betty cleaned it up a bit but it was still no place to live.

At this time my father was very frail. In his nineties, he was well taken care of by Norman Bentti and his wife, Hilja, two wonderful people. Norman did the driving, took care of the house and yard, and Hilja cooked and cleaned. Both of them babied my father outrageously. Dad said that in his whole life he'd never had it so good but he hungered to see his lake again. "Just one more time," he said over and over again.

So my brother Joe and I decided to get a new road in to our lakes and to build a fine new cabin on the point opposite Herman's Rock. Katy was disappointed in that choice; she wanted it built at her special place on the second lake, but that was impossible because of the expense entailed. Besides, I wanted the new road to come near the old cabin, hoping that some day I could rescue it from the shambles it had become.

The road they bulldozed followed the old wagon trail to where it climbed the steep hill, but then it ran west at the base of the ridge to the beaver dam, then up three smaller inclines to the big hardwoods and the lake, passing within only a hundred yards of the old cabin. It was hard to see the giant cedars and hemlocks being cut down on the point where I had so often slept as a youth, but they had to go. How raw the place looked when the bulldozer leveled off the clearing for the cabin site.

The man we selected to build the new cabin was Ivar Oman, the best "log butcher" in the U.P., according to Norman. The term is honorary, not derogatory. Anyone can build a shack but a log butcher is a notable craftsman. Ivar was getting old, but when we told him to make this cabin his masterpiece and that we didn't care how long it took or how much it cost, his eyes sure lit up. "How big a cabin?" he asked.

We told him to make it 24 by 36 feet with large double windows on the north, east and south side so we could see the lake from each of them. It should be one room without partitions and built of pine logs. We wanted a very large Heatilator fireplace that would take four-foot logs and be built of local rocks. We hoped he could construct four bunks also out of pine that would sleep twelve people. (We knew the grandchildren were coming.) Katy desired built-in cupboards of knotty pine and a long box under the south window for storage and where people could sit at the long table we'd bring down from the old cabin. We needed a well and a sink with a pump. (No more hauling water from the lake!) He should leave room for a propane gas stove and refrigerator, and install three pairs of gas mantle lamps.

Ivar, of course, couldn't handle the long, heavy logs by himself so Norman and his son, John, and his brother-in-law Alden Mattson helped with the heavy work. But Ivar was the boss! It was he who scribed the logs, then, with some ancient tools I'd never seen, chiseled them so the log above would fit perfectly into the one below. To see the old man eyeing those logs, whittling off a tiny projection, fitting and refitting them, was to see a real craftsman at work. He labored very slowly and very carefully with a lot of discussion and time off for his pipe and coffee. This was to be his cabin of cabins and he wanted it right!

All in all, it took two years (1968-1970) before it was finished and furnished, the men working all the summer months, and Ivar building the bunks, cupboards and other things during the winter at his house. In addition to the main cabin, they also built another smaller one to serve as a sauna or storage building. And, of course, they erected an outhouse hidden in the trees behind it, yet with a good view of the lake.

Big Cabin

Katy and I were there when Norman and Hilja drove my father up to see his lakes again. He was then 94 and failing fast but I could tell he was delighted. All he said, however, was, "You kids shouldn't have spent all that money but I'm glad you did." On their way back, Norman drove up the little side road to the old cabin but Dad didn't want to get out. Norman said he reminisced a lot about The Regulars and the old times in camp and the fun he'd had there. Dad never saw it again, dying that next winter.

Ivar died that next year too, but not before he managed to come up when I was in the new cabin with my family. We gave him coffee and cookies and a lot of appreciation. Before the old man left he went all around the inside and then the outside examining everything very carefully. "Yah, good!" he said, "Very good job! That cabin she will last one hundred year!" He told us to be sure to put a new coating on the roof every five years even if it didn't need it. We have done so.

Becoming A Grandfather

The new cabin was completed just in time, because within just a few years a veritable explosion of grandchildren occurred. Joe and Betty had two; Katy and I had nine. Every summer there were scheduling problems because our six families all wanted to be there in July and August when the flies had subsided. Nevertheless, by doubling up at different times we enjoyed ourselves despite the difficulties.

I wish I could recapture the joys of having my little grandchildren up at our lakes. To walk, hand in hand with them up the road under the huge trees, to let them lead me as we walked the old trails, to know again with younger eyes the marvels of moss and rocks and woods flowers was an experience beyond compare. They too, as my children and Katy and I had done, played and splashed in the waves naked as the dawn.

On one corner of the cabin we had a little camp bell, and when the grandchildren rang it I had to chase them around until they found sanctuary on Mr. Toad's Hill. The little girls built feeding stations for Manchester and the other chipmunks; the boys fished constantly or tried to catch frogs and minnows, or chased the squealing girls. They called my wife Gramma Katy and me MBG for Monkey Business Grampa. I tried to live up to the name.

Jamie and Jonathan

On the terrace just east of the cabin is a circle of stumps called Woodhenge, and in the middle of it is the fire pit. Each stump has a grandchild's name on it and at dusk each night they would find their stump and sit with us by the fire as their parents had done years before. Again, like their parents, when the mystery and sounds of the night spooked them, they'd run into the cabin, climb into their bunks and pull the covers over their little heads lest the woods monsters get them. How they squealed and giggled!

Just a few more memories of those years with the grandchildren: Jody, John's eldest, created a sanctuary on the beautiful point at the entrance to the south bay. Under a tall pine and on a great slab of granite covered with brown pine needles she built seats and tables and a feeding station for the chippies. Neither of her brothers was permitted there but once she honored me with an invitation to supper: lake water and pine cones. Gravely, I partook. Her sister, Julie, left her mark by printing messages in crayola on the bed slats above the lower bunks: "Good morning," "Sh! Time to go to sleep," and others.

Kelly Krill, Sue's daughter, at the age of four was not only beautiful but imperative. "MBG," she ordered. "We're going to play Peter and the Wolf. I'm Peter and you're the wolf. Go behind the shed, poke your neck out, and then I'll hit you with a stick and you run away crying. But, Grampa, be sure to come back."

The Safety of the Bunk

Jennifer Ann Squires, Cathy's daughter, and I had a special relationship which continues to this day. As a child she was very sensitive about being too short, so I invented VLB (Very Little Bear) who lived in a hole between the roots of a giant yellow birch, just up the hill from the cabin. Very Little Bear wrote Jennifer birch bark notes which she in turn answered. "Pookoo," he wrote, "It's no fair. It's no fair! Why do I have to be the smallest bear in the forest? Tell me how I can get bigger like the other bears." She wrote back that he should eat lots of peanut butter and jelly sandwiches or get some porcupine apples from the Porcupine Mountains. Once I prepared a tape recording and hid the recorder behind the tree before I led her to VLB's hole. For just a moment Pookoo's eyes were very wide until she heard the recorder click and found the machine. And hugged me! Even now, though she is very mature, both of us always look in the bear hole every time we go up there - and always find a note.

Jamie and Jonathan, John's sons, were fishing fools and I marveled at their patience. Since at first they were unable to go in the boat alone, I became their constant companion and mentor. The boys caught a lot of bass every day. To escape their constant begging me to take them out in the boat and to have some moments by myself, I'd often arise before dawn, have some coffee over an outdoor fire, then try to sneak away to do some fly fishing. Rarely was I successful. "Can I come too, Grampa? Can I come too?" Of course! But it was fun to see their excitement when they hooked a big fish. "Grampa, it's a hawg! It's Moby Dick!" It wasn't but I was a boy again with them.

Returning from the Very Little Bear's Hole

Much as my wife and I enjoyed having our children and theirs with us, there were times when we both felt we had lost something very precious. The deep quiet of the wilderness was gone and with it the great peace and serenity. There were just too many people around; there was just too much commotion. Every time I heard one of their dogs bark I winced. During the brief intervals between guests we could recapture the mystery of a lonely lake in the forest but soon another batch of happy, squealing kids would arrive. Yes, it was a fine, big cabin, a very comfortable one, but often it seemed very crowded.

I think they felt that way too because one day Sue and her family decided to clean up the old cabin. Ruthlessly for a week they worked at the project, throwing out the rusty old wood range, hauling out old mattresses, sweeping the floors and walls. When they finished, the place was very clean and very bare but it was still uninhabitable. There was just too much decay, too many holes. Without chairs or tables or mattresses, it was no place to live.

When I tried to get Norman to fix up the cabin he refused. And so did some other men I contacted. "No, Cully," they said when they looked it over. "That old shack's too far gone. We won't take your money. It's shot! Burn it down and build another one." I didn't want another one; I wanted my old cabin with all its fine memories.

So in 1972 I got two master carpenters, Tony Dykhouse and Jack Gesmundo, who had fixed up my old farmhouse in Kalamazoo, to go north to rebuild it. Dubious at first because of my description of what had to be done, Tony made a flying visit to look it over. "You'll need new bottom logs all around and some of the others replaced," he reported. "We'll have to put in a new floor, new corner posts and door frame and patch the roof. I also suggest that we put a new window in front so you'll have more light. Are you sure you want us to do it?"

I told him I did but that I didn't want that window, that I wanted the old cabin to look just like it did when I was a boy, and I didn't care how much it would cost. That September the two men spent two weeks on the job and I was delighted when I saw it at deer season. A perfect job! They'd even used the old door to make a table, put in a new stovepipe for the box stove, and caulked the seams between every log. That deer season I slept there every night and the cabin was so tight I had to fire up only once, whereas in the big cabin we always had to replenish the fire three or four times. I could hardly wait for summer to come so I could show it to Katy.

That summer, however, I was a visiting professor at the University of Montana so we didn't get to the lakes until late in August. Meanwhile, in July my brother Joe and his wife, Betty, and their son's family stayed at the big cabin. One hot afternoon while the latter were sleeping with the door wide open after their long trip north, Joe and Betty went fishing. As they approached the dock on their return they saw a big bear heading for that door. "I pulled hard for the dock," Joe said, "and told Betty to stay in the boat but to turn it around, that I was going to try to scare the bear away, but if I couldn't bluff him I'd be back to the boat fast. I took one of the oars, then ran around the corner of the cabin waving it and yelling at the top of my lungs. Well the bear was scared, but good, and ran up the hill as though the devil himself was after him. I found out later that it was one of the garbage dump bears at the state park that had been causing trouble there. They'd trapped it and released it at the headwaters of Wabeek Creek. They told me to get a rifle and shoot it if it returned but it stayed away from then on. I guess my act must have been convincing." The two babies, Trey and Christy, aged one and three, never woke up.

Bear

Up at the lakes we always saw bear signs each summer: their tracks, their black droppings, and the stumps they had torn apart to get the ants that were their salt and pepper. Once I had tried to take a picture of a cub high up in a tree, until the mother at its base chased me away. My first wood and canvas canoe that I'd left on the beach across the lake was wrecked completely by a bear while I was out exploring, perhaps because of its fish smell and from the bear's tracks it must have been a very large one. Sometimes at night we'd hear a bear wrestling with the garbage can by the doorway and one morning we found it gone, only to discover it still intact back of the outhouse, possibly because we'd tied the cover on tightly with rope. I still wonder how bears carry garbage cans. They stopped pestering us, however, when we began putting our fish entrails out on Herman's Rock in the middle of the lake. Herman, the seagull, approved.

Katy was overjoyed that summer when at last she got to the old cabin. "Now we can have a second honeymoon," she said, as she again wreathed the windows with ground pine. Going to Ishpeming, she bought new kitchen chairs, mattresses and other things, including a new red checkered tablecloth. Even before one of our families arrived we moved in. It was very, very good to sit outside again by a little night fire, then return to the old cabin to lie there with our arms around each other.

Rainbow On a Dark Day

Because we now had no cooking stove in the old cabin, we took all of our meals in the big cabin which meant, of course, that soon Katy was doing all the cooking for everyone. So I bought a Coleman camp stove and lantern and from then on we ate by ourselves except on special occasions. While we spent a lot of time at the big cabin with the grandchildren, it was good to be able to be alone with each other when we so wished.

That summer when my son, John, was staying at the new cabin, he built a dock that I doubted would survive the first spring breakup, but it survived for some years. Tied to it were our two boats, a big aluminum boat that my brother-in-law, Sam Dibble, had bought for us after he blew a hole in the aluminum pram with a cherry bomb one fourth of July, and a fiberglass rowboat that Joe and I had purchased. The canoe we kept on the sandy beach below the old cabin, so Katy and I could use it on our evening trips around the lake. The old pram we carried to the third lake so we could catch chub minnows for pike bait.

During those early years of the seventies the bass and pike fishing were so excellent we had Norman build a fish box to hold them and it was almost always full. Then about 1979 a great fish kill occurred one spring and the shoreline was full of dead perch. Soon afterward the number of pike diminished markedly, and by 1982 we rarely caught one. Why the bass did not also decline, I do not know. In the last few years, however, the pike have shown a remarkable increase. Indeed, Joe caught a big one on a fly last summer and several of us have had our leaders broken off, so perhaps old Moby Dick or his progeny still swim the lakes. I'll try for him again next summer.

When all the children and grandchildren left, Katy and I usually moved back to the big cabin because of its conveniences, though I always took my mandatory afternoon nap in the old cabin. One year a pair of flying squirrels entranced us by gliding down from the big cedars to the chipmunk feeding stations. They'd fill their cheeks, then climb the trees to do it over and over again. Rarely did they miss their target. The performance usually occurred just before dusk and then I'd go out fishing one last time, returning when I saw the flames in the fire pit or the candle in the window and Milove there beside them.

How I loved being out on that lonely lake at sundown. Still as black glass without a ripple on its surface, I watched the reflections of trees creep across the lake toward me until the far shore was just a dark sihouette. Many of the sunsets were spectacular with great masses of red and orange clouds outlined in black or white. Those very long U.P. evenings lasting until eleven o'clock are not seen Down Below.

The big cabin's outhouse sits in the deep woods about fifty feet east of the storage cabin. It is a good one, a two-holer with a wide swinging door which, when open, affords a good view of the shimmering lake. We keep it pretty clean and it has little of the usual privy smell because each person who uses it dumps a cupful of ashes or lime into the hole when done. Also, once or twice a week we empty a pail of water into it and dig it out about every four years.

The old cabin never had an outhouse. Behind it was a peeled log between two trees and a coffee can with toilet paper in it. I liked it, liked to do my daily duty in the open air with the breezes blowing down my legs. Eric Niemi, Tioga's old hermit, didn't have an outhouse either. He said he didn't want to be a chicken cooped up in its own crap.

But Katy had other ideas. Sitting on that bare log made her feel vulnerable. "The chipmunks look at me," she complained. Refusing to use the log, she would make the long trip up the side road then down the main road to the big cabin, then back to the new outhouse, a distance that was precarious when the urge was strong. So I made her a potty out of an old water pail covered with a piece of an old stove top that had the right sized hole in it. Even though I garnished it with moss, Katy used it only once and that in desperation. "Cut me a short-cut trail to the new outhouse, Cully," she demanded, so I did.

It was a mistake. The granchildren loved that blazed trail dearly. It made them feel as though they were walking in the great forest yet in no danger of getting lost, and besides Grampa and Grandma were at the other end of it. So they came and came. Jamie said he'd seen three bears on the way; Jody had been scared by a wolf; Susannah had heard a mountain lion. Excitedly they made it up to the safety of the old cabin to climb into our bunks and squeal with triumph. But our privacy was gone.

I suppose we could have gotten their parents to forbid their frequent invasions, or perhaps we could have, but we enjoyed having them come. Besides, my grandson Jamie had taught me a lesson some time before.

He'd been chasing his sister Julie around the big cabin threatening to maim her with a big club when I interfered. "No!"I yelled. "No! You can't do that!" Jamie dropped the club and wept. "Grampas mustn't say no," he said. "Grampas can't say no." I never said it again.

So I decided I'd just have to build another cabin, one so far away that we wouldn't ever be disturbed. By this time I'd purchased the east half of the third lake to supplement my father's small holding on it and to keep others from buying it when I heard it was for sale. Perhaps that was where the third cabin should be erected. Certainly it was inaccessible enough, so I hiked over there to look it over. Yes, we could get a road bulldozed to it from the east from the Ox-Bow on Wabeek Creek, but when I thought it over I couldn't bring myself to do it. I couldn't bear to spoil its pristine beauty. We needed one lake that was untouched and wild.

Then why not build a cabin on the second lake at that special place where Katy always wanted one? Unfortunately, that would mean that we'd have to bulldoze a new road around the south and west of our lake and spoil those lovely hardwoods. No! I refused to even consider it.

On our way home that summer we stopped overnight at Boyne Falls and there I saw a firm that would erect a prefabricated pine log cabin anywhere and was really tempted. Though the one I wanted seemed very expensive, I'd just received a very fat royalty check from one of the publishers of my textbooks. Believing that money is only good when you can despise or spend it, I picked out the one I wanted. It was 24 by 32 feet, had two bedrooms and a big living room and kitchen area, hardwood floors and casement windows. They would deliver and erect it, but only if I could have all of the material transported to the second lake site from the clearing by the big cabin. At first that seemed impossible. We would have to bring the big sections across on the rowboats, then down the outlet channel, and carry them up the hill, a very steep one. The only way it could be done was to get a lot of help and move all the stuff early in the spring in high water time.

But it was done. When, on Memorial Day in 1974, four of us and Norman arrived at the big cabin, we found the clearing half covered with a mountain of lumber and sections of the new cabin. It seemed crazy to think we could transport all of it across to the second lake but we did. Balancing those big sections on top of the rowboats, lugging them up the steep hill day after day drained us of all energy. Once Tim said, "You know, of course, that this is insane." It was, but somehow the job got completed.

Two weeks later, a crew of men from the factory came up to put it together, and a week later they were finished. One of them told Norman that they'd built cabins all over the country but never one in such an isolated and beautiful place.

By the time I brought my wife up to see the new cabin in late July the lake level was so low we couldn't go down the outlet, so we parked the canoe near Birch Point and walked to the second lake from there. Katy gasped when the new cabin suddenly appeared, its new pine logs shining in the sun yet closely surrounded by white birch, pine and fir trees. I know how she felt. Even now after many years I always get her sense of disbelief. To find in the deep forest a shiny, tall cabin is to doubt one's senses. "Oh, Cully," Katy exclaimed. "It's magical. Some sorcerer has waved a wand and said 'Behold!'" She hesitated when she touched the doorknob as though it couldn't be real.

When she entered she gasped again as she saw the high-pitched ceiling and the big picture window that gives a magnificent view of the lake. "What a place to see sunsets! I'm dreaming," she said, "but don't wake me up." We sat on the wide porch for a long time and when she descended the front steps she kissed the ferns and moss. I was remembering too.

From that time onward our scheduling and privacy problems were solved. Only one summer were all the cabins full and that was my fault. Feeling patriarchal, I'd made the mistake of inviting all of my children and grandchildren to come at the same time, to assemble the whole clan. Although everyone had a fine time, there were just too many of them. We never tried that again.

New Cabin on Second Lake

The following year I taught again at the University of Montana, and because Katy and I stayed in a little cabin on Rock Creek I had some of the best fly fishing for trout I've ever known. Nevertheless, I couldn't wait to get back to the U.P.

I should have waited. When we arrived at the lakes the air was polluted by the angry snarl of chain saws, the crashing of trees, and the rumble of logging trucks. The Mead Corporation, a large timber company that owned all the land east of us, had been selectively cutting the big hardwood all winter and the operation was about concluded. When I hiked over there I felt sick. The great maples and birch and hemlocks through which The Regulars and I had roamed so often were piles of slashings. Skid roads scarred the forest floor. For some reason they had not touched any of the trees along the east shore of the lake, so that still looked as beautiful as ever but oh, the nasty sound of those chain saws! Even at the new cabin on the second lake we couldn't escape hearing them spoil the silence.

Once, while there (and we only stayed a week) I was sitting on a newly fallen birch tree trying to keep my fingers out of my ears when a man came down the road. Representing another logging company, he wanted to buy the timber rights to our land. When I gave him an immediate no, he tried to persuade me. "I've cruised your lands," he said. "You have some valuable trees that should be cut down now because soon they'll fall down anyway, like the one you're sitting on which might be worth fifty dollars for veneer. And you have some bird's-eye maple worth even more. This is a climax forest that would be all the better for some pruning." I told him I didn't need the money but even if I did I wouldn't let anyone cut down my trees because they were my friends. If they grew old and fell down, well, I'd do so too some day, and I hoped that my children would scatter my dust there so I could be reincarnated as moss or wildflowers or perhaps even as a birch tree like this one. The man didn't argue any more; he just shook his head at my benightedness and left.

It was fascinating to see how soon the forest recovered from its rape. Now, fifteen years later, the slashings have disappeared into the earth; the logging roads are overgrown; the stumps have disintegrated. It is still wilderness. Only someone who had known the giant trees of the past would know what had happened and, of course, our own land has the big trees still.

One afternoon the next summer Katy and I were sitting in the big cabin and she was sewing mushrooms so they could be hung from the top of the windows to dry. We'd found a lot of oyster mushrooms that morning sitting in layers on dead maple logs, too many for our scrambled eggs and steak, so we were drying them to have at home the next winter. I was jotting down some notes for tales that would eventually become a Northwoods Reader, although at the time I had no thoughts of publication. I just wanted to put down on paper my memories of the zany characters I'd known in Tioga as a boy, so my children and their children could enjoy them too. My writing was going slowly because I kept looking at the lake which changes constantly. That afternoon it seemed covered with floating islands of

96

frosted glass. Then came a knock on the door.

It was Dennis Visserink, a timber cruiser and forester for the Mead Corporation, he said. I stiffened. To hell with the Mead Corporation! But he was a charming young fellow and won us over immediately. He said he was sorry that Mead felt it was time to cut the ripe trees because he loved the untouched forest too. He also said he was glad I refused the offer to cut our timber. And then he threw the bomb! He and two other Mead foresters, Tim Bulema and Bob Carpenter, were planning to erect a hunting cabin on the bluff above the sandy beach on the east end of our lake. They wouldn't bother us, he said, but he felt we ought to know. I found it difficult to be civil when he left.

Again we were being invaded. Much of my love for the lake was due to its isolation and now we would have to share it with others. Damn their hides! I'd known, of course, that Mead owned the east shoreline of our big lake because my father long before had tried to buy it and had been refused. It was then company policy never to sell any lake frontage. I too had tried several times to buy it, but in vain.

In time, everything worked out well. The three young foresters worked hard putting up their cabin of pine boards, scrounging most of the materials. Dennis said it only cost them $500 in biting money. Though not very attractive, it has a fine view of the lake, and now one can hardly see it up there on the hill.

Moreover it now is rarely used. For a few years the Mead boys hunted from it every November but, discovering there weren't many deer, they found better places. At first they occasionally brought up their attractive young wives to spend a weekend swimming, but now they seldom do and that is too bad because we enjoyed their visits.

In 1976, just before we came north, someone broke into the big cabin and our storage cabin by slamming a big chunk of maple into the doors. There's very little crime in the U.P. and it was certainly almost unknown in Tioga, but that spring a lot of hunting cabins and summer cottages were raided. The new automobile road into our lake had made us vulnerable for the first time. Norman was sure who did it but had no proof, but finally when a man from Tioga went to jail the stealing stopped. We lost only saleable articles, outboard motors, binoculars, an expensive fly rod and some other things.

Someone suggested that I put up "No Trespassing" signs but I refused. As Norman said, the only ones they keep out are honest men. Besides, I've always hated those signs. Instead I got the Mead boys to put up a suspended iron gate across the road just before the steep hill. This is padlocked except when we are in residence. I hate to see that gate but at least it makes a thief think twice about having to carry his loot so far, and we've had no trouble since.

Let me give one more account of winter-wonderland. John, Tim, and Tim's father, Del Squires, were with me at deer hunting time when it was very cold, even too cold for the suckling pig I'd brought up with me.

The night before we cooked it we had blown out the candles and were sitting by the fire when someone looked out of the south window. "Hey!" he exclaimed. "Come look! There's a bunch of deer right here in the yard." Indeed there was. Seven or eight of them were wandering around right in front of the cabin, sniffing the car, and eating some of the apples we'd put by the flagpole. It was too dark to see horns or to shoot but two of them were very large and probably bucks. They hung around for almost half an hour and one big doe walked around the cabin, peering in at us with her nose against the north window and waving her ears. Nothing like that had ever happened before, nor has since.

The Gate

We were up before daylight to find the clearing literally covered with deer tracks as we built a big fire in the fire pit where we planned to roast the suckling pig. While the others went hunting, I contrived forked sticks and a spit on which to turn the critter. None of us had ever roasted a pig before but we knew we had to have a lot of coals so I kept splitting small wood all that morning as well as dumping two bags of charcoal on the fire.

Just about noon, when the coals were looking good, I heard a fusillade of shots from over by Porcupine Bluff and felt certain that John or Tim or Del had got a buck. But no, in they came looking sheepish. Yes, they'd seen the herd of the night before. No, they hadn't hit one of them. The hex that Katy and Cathy had invoked whenever they saw a deer in summertime had been too potent. It was time for a cup of coffee.

Winter Spruce

It was also time for them to spell me in tending that damned pig, mending the coals, turning the spit that skewered it. Then shortly after lunch it began to snow terribly hard with flakes so big we could hardly see the dock. First we erected a tent of branches over the fire pit, then later a V of the corrugated steel sheets used for roofing. The wind blew constantly; the snow kept coming down; we burned up most of our kindling and small wood; the pig turned black. At Happy Hour I tried to poke a fork in the carcass but couldn't. Finally, at 9:30 that evening we brought in the suckling pig, laid it on a plank with an apple in its snout, and began carving. It sure looked good but when we managed to cut it open all we found was red, raw flesh. "Well," said John. "It was a beautiful thought!" We carried it out to the flagpole for the ravens and opened a can of pork and beans.

After I retired from my professorship at the university I was able to get up to our lakes more often. Several times I came alone; twice my brother Joe and I spent wonderful weeks of companionship there; but always Katy and I returned for months each summer. Each visit provided new experiences. For two years a pair of three-toed arctic woodpeckers joined us, chipping out a nesting hole in a big cedar by the dock. Completely unafraid, they went about their business of laying four white eggs and hatching their young. If we came too close, they made a curious rattling noise as a warning when we came near.

Then there was the summer of the bat. I've always liked bats, those odd little mammals with human faces, big ears and leathery wings.

We've always had them at our lakes, swooping low over the water catching insects with their sonar, but that summer a lot of them had bedded down in the eaves of the big cabin and all day long we could hear them twittering in the northwest corner. That was all right but then they began to appear inside the cabin every night. Katy didn't like them one bit as they swooped around her. She'd cover her head with an apron or towel fearing that they'd get in her hair, though of course they never did. "Cully, get that thing out of here!" she'd command and her hero would try. It wasn't easy. A bat will zag when you expect it to zig. After trying in vain to swat it with a broom, I finally won the battle with a fine-meshed minnow net, released the bat outside, went to bed, and there it was again. I closed the fireplace damper; back it came. Bats only need a hole no bigger than a pencil to invade. Not until Norman squirted some Raid into their nest in the eaves did they stop pestering us. He said he heard them coughing, and Norman is an honest man.

Deer

One summer we did a lot of excavating around the site of the old logging camps in the south bay, finding chains, peavies, canthooks and pieces of an old stove. The place was so overgrown we could barely discern the outlines of the main camp and horse barn, but with a metal detector we spent days investigating it.

One afternoon as I was walking around the north end of the lake I saw something blue on the forest floor. It was the top of a blue enameled coffee pot, still intact but with the bottom rusted out. Near it I also found some mounds arranged in a square that looked as though they were the remains of a little cabin, but I couldn't be sure. When I told Cathy and Tim about it they spent most of one of their vacations excavating the site. Yes, it was a cabin, probably a trapper's cabin, because there were no pieces of window glass and because it was a small one only about eight feet by eight feet. Cathy and Tim found pieces of an old cast iron stove, rusted forks and spoons, a cup, and a tiny little object that looked as though it were a lamp that could be worn on a cap. I have been unable to unearth any information about the man who lived there so many years ago, but I feel a deep kinship with him. He too roamed the land around my lakes.

Lamp from Old Trapper's Cabin Site

Katy and I always enjoyed watching Herman the seagull out on his white rock where we put our fish entrails and edible garbage. What a pig he was! When another gull appeared he gave battle, filling the air with harsh cries until it was driven away. He was king of that white castle but Herman got his comeuppance, however, when a great blue heron arrived. The gull would screech and flutter its wings but the heron would just stand there motionless, then suddenly give Herman a sharp peck with its long bill to call his bluff. And then it would eat everything on the rock. How Herman swore when he returned to find the rock bare. We also had a large bald eagle that day after day chased Herman away and fed on his victuals. What a magnificent bird! To see it soaring above with those great wings, then swoop down to its landing is unforgettable. Herman never tried to bluff the eagle but left immediately and didn't return for several days.

Bald Eagle and Raven Feeding

Growing Old

When I was in my seventies I no longer hunted or fished so hard, nor did I gallop over the hills and far away. It was enough just to sit beside my wife looking out at the lake in its varying moods, or to find a grassy spot in the hardwoods where I could lie and watch the big branches waving in the wind. Often at these times there came ideas for the tales that eventually became my Northwoods Readers. I'd started writing them because my grandchildren liked the stories I told them of my youth in Tioga. Mainly, I related incidents from my own childhood with, as Poobah in the Mikado said when accused of lying, "a little corroborative detail intended to give artistic verisimilitude to a bald and unconvincing narrative." The girls liked the one about the bat that got into my Grandmother Gage's hat and the one about Mrs. Murphy and her pig; the boys loved my tales about Old Blueballs and P.P. Polson; they all enjoyed anything I told them about my Grandpa Gage. "Tell me another story, Grandpa; tell me another story," they'd beg. I had no thought of ever publishing them at the time, but wrote them down so my children could read them to their own children some day.

Oddly, I never could write them when I was staying at our lakes. Once I took my typewriter up there and never touched it because I didn't want to waste a moment of enjoyment, but at night I'd think of more stories to tell. I seem to have to wait until I get back Down Below and then write so I can get through the miserable winters and return again to the land I love.

In the nineteen-eighties the illusion that I was still a boy in the great woods began to leave me. I was growing old. So was Norman, he said, as he asked to be relieved of his caretaking duties. That was hard to believe because he still looked as lean and tough as ever. Finn men never seem to age much, perhaps because of all their saunas. Our new caretaker, Rich Waisanen, the son of Iggy, my old friend, is a big man with muscles on his muscles, who works in the mines but lives in the woods as much as he can, and has a hunting camp on the east branch of the Wabeek. He has added much to our life. How he manages to put in and haul out the new heavy wooden floating docks each year I do not know. He cuts our wood and watches over our cabins and shoots the deer that we miss.

The old cabin was almost seventy years old and in much better shape than I was, perhaps because no one had rebuilt me. Heart attacks, phlebitis, blackouts and diabetes had taken their toll, but better to die from the bottom up than from the top down! When I was able to get to the lakes, however, I rarely had any trouble. Oh, there were a few times, as when I was blazing a new trail on a hot afternoon, I found my face in the forest floor and my heart going crazy, but usually I was well and full of peace and serenity. Behind the old cabin there's a beautiful pointed rock about six feet tall covered with soft moss, my healing rock. Whenever I arrived, I'd go there, sit beside it with my face against the moss, and feel the healing come over me. Pyramid power? But it was harder to walk the forest trails, to leap from rock to rock, or to climb over a windfall. I wrote a little poem to my old bones.

Upon Arising
Old bones! Old bones! Creaky old bones!
Skin sack: Pain sack,
Full of aches and groans.
Like Sister Alice Rose Marie,
Black in habit and hosiery,
Tolling the beads of her rosary,
I scan my torso from skull to knee,
Spotting the spots of my misery.
Old bones! Old bones!
Damned old bones!
Yet I'll sing a small song to greet the day,
Knowing some beauty will come my way
To compensate for the pain I pay
In my old bones. Old bones!
Bloody old bones!

But Milady Katy wasn't growing old at all. Each year she became more beautiful. Full of energy, she walked the lake trails for me, always returning with interesting accounts of her experiences. Herky, our springer spaniel, had suddenly confronted a deer and chased it down the road only to skid to a stop when he realized the big animal wasn't a rabbit. That sort of thing! Always she brought back a treasure she had found: a new mushroom to identify, an Indian pipe, a cardinal flower from the swamp, a handful of blue gentians.

How I loved to see her just walking around the cabin, or hearing her as she sang the old songs. I loved her hands, beautiful hands, gnarled by years of serving others. When I put my arm around her slim waist or when she put her bare arms around my neck, I always felt the old exquisite thrill. Just to sit beside her on the stumps of Woodhenge was to know how blessed I had been.

But then there came a year, in 1982, when a drastic change occurred. Milove lost her sparkle and gaiety. It was hard for her to walk though she drove herself to go to the old cabin each day. She found it hard to cook and even harder to eat anything. Not that she ever complained. Often I could see her pretending to be happy so I wouldn't worry. Occasionally she would try to tend the little garden where she'd transplanted arbutus and other woods flowers, but always she returned completely exhausted.

When I proposed that we leave immediately for home to see our physician, Katy opposed it strongly. No! She needed more time up there and besides she wanted to wait until Elizabeth, her eldest granddaughter, and husband, Andy Amor, arrived. Finally, she acceded. I'd hoped that when she got to our 130-year-old brick farmhouse, she'd feel better, but that didn't happen. Our doctor examined her briefly and ordered a tomogram that revealed a large mass in her abdomen. When they operated the next day, they found an ovarian cancer too large to be operable so they just sewed her up again, saying that chemotherapy was her only chance for survival.

I won't go into the details of the two terrible years that ensued. I did the cooking and cleaning and cared for her night and day. Through all those long months she was gallant and courageous. Never did I hear her say, "Why me?" When I told her how much I admired her bravery, she said, "Don't admire me, Cully. Just love me." I don't think I ever loved her more.

Our Last Trip

The next summer I had no interest whatsoever in going north and was surprised and shocked when she presented me with two plane tickets to Marquette. She said she just had to go back to our lakes one more time. She had to see the old cabin again. I protested but anything she wanted she could have. By programming her hospital sessions of chemotherapy so she could lengthen the period between them, we did have two final bittersweet weeks together at our lakes. Before we left she carved these words on a big Indian slate: "I'm only a smile away."

She died the next August.

This book should probably end right here but there is just a bit more to say. In September my son John drove me up to the lakes to do some of my grieving. Some of it. My healing rock didn't help much and after I got home I found our old house very, very empty.

But life goes on, a life that has a big hole in it which shows no sign of shrinking but I try to live around it with some grace. Writing more Northwoods Readers has helped and so have my trips northward. I've managed to get to the cabins every summer and every deer season. Everything up there has changed; yet everything remains the same. Herman sits on his white rock; the old cabin holds me in its arms; the forest and lakes lift my spirit. Children and grandchildren join me there and last summer at the cabin on the second lake we watched a mother moose feeding on Katy's white water lilies, then swim, with her calf across to the south shore. The loons give their long wail at eventide and I find some peace. That other love affair, the one I've had with my beloved U.P. still continues. "I'll be back again, old cabin."

Moose by Second Lake

We at Avery Color Studios thank you for purchasing this book. We hope it has provided many hours of enjoyable reading.

Learn more about Michigan and the Great Lakes area through a broad range of titles that cover mining and logging days, early Indians and their legends, Great Lakes shipwrecks, Cully Gage's Northwoods Readers (full of laughter and occasional sadness), and full-color pictorials of days gone by and the natural beauty of this land.

Also available are beautiful full-color placemats and note stationery.

To obtain a free catalog, please call (800) 722-9925 in Michigan, or (906) 892-8251, or tear out this page and mail it to us. Please tape or staple the card and put a stamp on it.

PLEASE RETURN TO:

Avery Color Studios
Star Route - Box 275
Au Train, Michigan 49806
Phone: (906) 892-8251
IN MICHIGAN
CALL TOLL FREE
1-800-722-9925

Your complete shipping address:

_____

_____

_____

_____

Fold, Staple, Affix Stamp and Mail

_____

_____

_____

_____

Avery COLOR STUDIOS

Star Route - Box 275
AuTrain, Michigan 49806